BAD MONEY

L. J. DAVIS

ST. MARTIN'S PRESS · NEW YORK

To my mother, Eula J. Logsdon

Portions of this book have appeared, in slightly different form, in *Harper's,
Mother Jones,* and *Penthouse*.

BAD MONEY. Copyright © 1982 by L. J. Davis. All rights reserved. Printed in the
United States of America. No part of this book may be used or reproduced in any
manner whatsoever without written permission except in the case of brief
quotations embodied in critical articles or reviews. For information, address St.
Martin's Press, 175 Fifth Avenue, New York, N.Y. 10010.

Library of Congress Cataloging in Publication Data

Davis, L. J. (Lawrence J.)
  Bad money.

  1. Economic history—1945–   2. Finance
3. Bankruptcy.   4. Bank failure.   I. Title.
HC59.D393   332.7′5   81–21511
ISBN 0-312-06524-8   AACR2

First Edition

Contents

Acknowledgments

Like all writers, I have been helped in the composition of this book by many people, and hindered by a few. In the former category, I would like to single out Lewis H. Lapham, the former editor of *Harper's,* who sent me to hunt Libyans in Idaho and expressed no surprise when I announced that I had caught the Euromarket instead. If there are any credible passages in the following pages, Mr. Lapham is therefore the founder of the feast—and not incidentally, he is also the finest editor I have ever known. Any mistakes are mine alone, and I will take the rap for them.

Among other *Harper's* personnel, both past and present, who helped me on my way, I would like to thank David Sanford, Matthew Stevenson, David Doty, and Ashley Harvey, who did their level best to ensure that the language I wrote was English and that the numbers added up—always matters of no small concern when one is writing about money. At *Penthouse,* Jim Goode and Peter Bloch contributed their patience and ingenuity to the pursuit of David Rockefeller, the Chase Manhattan, and the imperiled $800 million; and Zena Klapper opened the pages of *Mother Jones* to a further discussion of the problem of the OPEC millions. Nor would the list be complete without a mention of Peter Iseman, who untangled the mystery of Prince Abdullah's wakeel and who acted as a powerful corrective force to the popular and mistaken notions (which I then shared) of the intentions and activities of the House of Saud.

My understanding of the enormous machinations of the Hunts would have been woefully incomplete without the splendid groundbreaking work done by Congressman Benjamin Rosenthal and the staff of his subcommittee on commerce, consumer, and monetary affairs, particularly the subcommittee's counsel, Barbara Timmer; as the silver crisis broke, their small corner of the government functioned exactly the way it was supposed to, and their documentation of the story is by far the clearest to have appeared. At Gannett News Service, Ralph Soda was out of the starting gate and in full cry after the Texans long before I entered the field, and his advice saved me many a false start. The inestimable Ernest Volkman also contributed his widow's mite of sound common sense, without which this undertaking might have been a good deal longer without being in the least bit better.

It was Diana Finch at St. Martin's Press who saw the possibilities of a book in my disorderly ruck of articles, and who kept me to my last with good cheer and intelligent guidance through thick, thin, and broken deadlines. Nor should my gimlet-eyed agent, Patricia Berens, be forgotten, for it was she who kept the groceries on the table while the book was taking shape.

Lastly, my family must be mentioned, particularly my wife, Barbara, and my elder son, Jeremy, who lent their encouragement and their ears, and who suffered through much tedious tabletalk on the subject of Eurodollars, petrodollars, IMF facilities, and backwardations; it is a miracle we survived.

Prologue:
J. P. Morgan Walks at Midnight

The decade of the seventies began with the largest business failure in American history, the collapse of the Penn Central railroad. It proceeded through the crisis of 1974–76, brightly illuminated by conflagrations at the Franklin National Bank, the largest banking failure in American history, and at the W. T. Grant department store chain, the largest mercantile failure. Then, just as the decade seemed to be dwindling out in a kind of pervasive sourness where nothing went right anymore, it came to a tidy close with a great market panic inspired by the attempt of a pair of eccentric Texas billionaires, fed up like the rest of us, to establish their own silver-based currency. It was also—in a way that touched the lives of almost everyone on the planet—the decade of OPEC, the Ayatollah, and the Chase Manhattan Bank. Meanwhile, the nation's bankers launched a concerted assault on the nation's bread and butter—not intending to, of course; they were simply trying to make a lot of money in a new way—and almost nobody noticed, including the bankers themselves. But as my old editor, Lewis H. Lapham, is fond of remarking, everything connects; a giant transportation combine, badly merged and badly managed, goes bankrupt. Nine years later, a shah develops a gallstone, an embassy is sacked and hostages are taken, and a bank saves itself $800 million. There is a unity to these events; they are part of an evolutionary process that it is the purpose of this book to explore.

It might be said of the art of high finance, as Talleyrand once said of government, that if the average citizen ever realized how meanly he is served, he would probably be pretty upset. As the United States sailed boldly forth to new adventures in the 1980s, its economy was in a shambles, its banking system had gone completely haywire, its currency was debased by inflation, and it seemed as though nobody in a position of power had the faintest idea of what the hell was going on. The great banks were generating new money—but not creating wealth, an important distinction—causing inflation in circumstances where, according to traditional economic thought, no inflation should exist. The banking system had, in fact, usurped a function that is supposed to belong exclusively to the government. The banks, not the government, controlled the supply of money, and much of the recent history of the West can be understood through a study of how this strange and fragile state of affairs came to pass.

The years immediately following World War II had witnessed a quiet but significant change in the way American business provided itself with the fuel of commerce in the form of money. It went into hock. While there is nothing about such a step that would curl the hair of a European plutocrat— European industries have long funded their activities with short-term debt, the way an average American citizen funds (or, anyway, used to fund) the purchase of a car—there was no useful American precedent for indebtedness on such a scale, and therefore no accepted wisdom. Traditionally, American business had paid for its undertakings out of accumulated profits, issues of new stock, and long-term, nonbank debt in the form of bond issues, stopping at the bankers' well only when these sources of funds were inadequate. Short-term bank credit, although in the aggregate large, played a relatively minor role in sound business strategy, being largely employed to speed the transfer of funds, to seize an opportunity, to effect an expansion, to make good a shortfall, or to gain certain tax advantages; it was a tactical and not a strategic instrument. But with abundant capital made available by a benign Federal Reserve in the immediate postwar years and later by the innovation of the bankers, American businessmen suddenly found themselves standing on the shores of a lake of money. Who can blame them for jumping in?

In the natural course of things, short-term indebtedness led to short-term debt rollovers—paying off the unexpired portion of a loan with a fresh, new loan—and the need for rollovers inevitably led to the invention of new financial instruments and institutions, all designed to expand the money supply. As the snowball grew larger, the whole undertaking began to resemble an increasingly frantic movement of money from one pocket to the other, debt covering debt and the devil take the Federal Reserve. In a complete reversal of common sense, the deeper a company went into hock, the more creditworthy it became, and the more it expanded, the greater its debt. Smaller competitors, less happily encumbered, fell by the wayside, giant retail chains grew ever larger, the commercial diversity of American life was slowly destroyed, and the lucky winners relied increasingly on the banks rather than on their entrepreneurial skills. All a company (and its debt) had to do was grow; it didn't even have to be particularly good at what it did. The result was a kind of fever-dream of increasingly hectic corporate mismanagement, and a growing danger that, sometime very soon, circumstances would combine to call everyone's bluff. When push comes to shove, if you have piled up a mountain of debt, there are only two things you can do with it. You can default on it, or you can pay it back. But meanwhile, the bankers had looked upon their handiwork and found it good, and they exported it abroad, into a vast, mad marketplace of their devising, the Euromarket, where whole countries could play the game. And soon, if the debts had been called, there wasn't enough money in the world to make them good.

In making my way through a battlefield so littered with corpses, I have been compelled to pick and choose among the victims. Some—Lockheed, for example, or the crisis in the utility companies in 1976—I have omitted because they are either redundant or lacking in depth and richness of detail. I have likewise chosen not to deal at length with the fate of the Franklin National Bank because its collapse was largely a matter of the outright criminality of its chief, the Italian financier Michele Sindona, and it is therefore an aberration. The crisis at Chrysler similarly gets short shrift—reluctantly, since it is a particularly telling example of the sins of short-term credit—but Chrysler's story is still not over.

Many things come together in the troubles at the Penn Central, at Grant, at the Chase, and in the thinking of the brothers Hunt—not only commercial paper, but a variety of highly questionable financial strategems, all of them rather frighteningly commonplace and all of them central to our present economic dilemma. The common thread that binds these institutions together is, of course, money; its increasing volatility, diminishing value, indispensability, and the tricks that can be played with it in the name of profit. But there is another thread as well, a history of fiduciary bungling on an almost cosmic scale. To explain how such a pass was arrived at, I have rung in a brief study of the treasure of OPEC (and where it went) and included a chapter—lacking, I fear, in a certain dash and color, but essential—on the workings of the Euromarket, without a proper understanding of which the working of the world's financial mechanism cannot be understood.

If this book can be said to have a hero, it is Junius Pierpont Morgan. I realize he is an unlikely choice; the old plutocrat has taken his knocks for seventy years now, and his memory has few friends. But if the choice is unlikely, it is also inevitable. Simply put, Morgan understood money and the structures money erects. Like most members of the human race, Morgan desired money; unlike many members of the human race, he attained it. Still, the accumulation of a fortune is not a particularly unusual act, and Morgan's black reputation rests elsewhere, in his attempts to impose order on the dangerously unruly struggles that characterized the classical age of American capitalism.

Like the great monopolists of the period, Morgan was acutely aware of the destructive aspects of uncontrolled competition; he was a banker, after all, deeply involved with the creation and preservation of wealth. As such, his thinking was a little different from that of the first Rockefeller, whose every waking hour was devoted to the domination of a particular industry in the name of lining his pockets with coin, but Rockefeller's greed and Morgan's conservative temperament brought them to the same conclusion at the end. The industrial revolution had not merely changed the rules of the game; it was playing a different game altogether. As understood by Adam Smith, competition encouraged a pleasing diversity in the marketplace and provided certain self-corrective checks to excess, dishonesty, and the concentration of power, but for Adam Smith's system to work at all, it had to function in Adam Smith's idealized eighteenth-century world, where God was an Englishman and enterprise was concentrated in the hands of artisans and shopkeepers.

That world no longer existed, if it ever had; it disappeared into the firebox of Mr. Watt's steam engine and was never seen again. By the 1890s, heavy industry had uncovered vast new resources and created vast new markets, resulting in enormous new concentrations of wealth in the hands of huge warring enterprises. Competition was no longer a genteel exercise in beggar-my-neighbor; beggar-my-neighbor it remained, but on a scale inconceivable to a mind that had never seen a railroad or a steel mill, because neither had existed. Wealth creates its own imperatives, or rather its quantity does. In the eighteenth century, it was a finite substance, something to be hoarded and deployed with caution, if at all.

In the nineteenth century, the world suddenly seemed very young again, and money seemed to spring up from the earth, like a crop.

We have forgotten what it was like to conquer a country, a continent, a world, with steam and money; we live again as men have usually lived, in an era of limits. When the great entrepreneurs of the last century clashed for markets, they did so on a heroic scale, putting each other's territories to the sword as though they were rival armies, squandering money as though there were no end to wealth. It was vastly entertaining, of course—but as Morgan understood with a clarity he carried with him to the grave, it was as wasteful as the warfare it resembled, and it was irrational. As a banker, as an Episcopalian, as a capitalist with an unusual amount of historical perspective (and with a keen sense of just how his contemporaries and posterity would misjudge him, he ironically named each of his yachts *Corsair),* he set out to impose order.

Morgan realized that when an industry reaches a certain point in its maturity, competition becomes wasteful and irrational, and orderly structures and clear sets of rules are required. Perhaps the answer was a monopoly, perhaps it was vertical integration, but if fresh wealth was to be created and capital conserved, a rational structure had to be imposed.

The rationalization of the business structure of a country is not only an economic act but a social one; it prevents needless duplication of facilities, deploys capital with a measure of efficiency, and keeps the paychecks coming with a certain regularity. If the mere accumulation of wealth is the only goal, there are many ways of going about the task, as the multinational bankers and conglomerateurs of our own distressed age have abundantly demonstrated; rational economic structures have more to do with the creation and preservation of wealth than with its distribution, and they owe more to pragmatism than to morality or doctrine. Morgan was by no means pure; like everybody else, he was trying to make a buck. Nor was he pursuing anything resembling a national economic policy. Unlike his enemies among the populists, Morgan was an old-fashioned, eighteenth-century mercantilist who happened to be the most powerful banker in the country, and his goal was to tighten up the machinery of wealth. Ironically, he soon found himself standing as inadvertent godfather to a whole body of regulatory legislation that made rational economic structures all but impossible.

The basic assumptions of the populist legislators were two: that competition was intrinsically good, and that large companies were inherently evil. It therefore made eminent sense for them to perpetrate a paradox. They passed legislation and established regulatory bodies designed to foster the competitive spirit, while at the same time they passed other legislation and instructed other regulatory bodies to enforce regulations that ignored market forces, changes in technology, vital national priorities, and the creation of rational structures, all in the name of foiling the ambitions of the giant corporations. In other words, they made anything resembling true competition impossible, while attempting to freeze the corporations in a subservient posture that in many cases made it impossible for them to evolve or react in the face of new challenges. One inevitable result, as the Penn Central chapter will make clear, was the stagnation and eventual collapse of the northeastern railroads. Another, even more invidious result was the effect all this regulation had on the entrepreneurial mind; since rational economic structures were now impossible, entrepreneurs set out to make money in ways that had little to do with making sense.

The change was slow in coming; two world wars and the Great Depression were compelling distractions. It wasn't until the go-go days of the 1960s that the archaic regulations of the populists combined with federal highway and mortgage policies to produce two strange new entities, the conglomerate and the suburban shopping mall, with effects that are easily discernible; no one is untouched by the collapse of the central cities and the slow death of the nation's heavy industry and its basic transportation system.

Since both conglomerates and the economic life of the

suburbs are somewhat evanescent affairs—the former designed to make money by passing through regulatory loopholes, the latter dependent on volatile shifts of population and governmental initiatives that have nothing to do with market forces (i.e., the building of highways with public funds in places already well served by privately capitalized railroads)—they are devoted to the generation of short-term profits rather than long-term capital formation. This brings us back to the central problem of the last third of the present century; the accumulation of the mountain of debt.

With heavy industry stagnating and its cash reserve depleted, it was compelled to live on credit, a good example being the Penn Central. Meanwhile, flush times in the government-created suburbs cried out for new retailing strategies. But with capital formation a very secondary consideration compared to immediate profit, the best source of funds for expansion lay in the creation of lines of credit, and one ends up with something like a W. T. Grant.

In order to keep older industries alive while funding the irrational new entities that had grown up in the interstices of law and accepted wisdom, new money had to be found. There's always a certain amount of new money in the system, of course; the Treasury and the Fed see to that. Unfortunately, there wasn't enough of it to feed the hunger created by irrational federal policies that had been promulgated in ignorance of both probable consequence and national monetary policies, and in the sixties the banks themselves went into the business of slipping through the regulatory net. They did so, in part, by exporting much of their business abroad, and by harnessing the nation's economic fate to the continued solvency and goodwill of the House of Saud and to the ability of a handful of right-wing dictatorships to avoid collective bankruptcy.

None of it made any sense, of course. The entire system was structured so that making sense was impossible. That distant low humming you hear is the sound of J. P. Morgan, rotating like a turbine in his grave.

1.

The Road to West Jockstrap

As Samuel Johnson might have said, the wonder of the Penn Central merger wasn't that it was done badly, but that it was done at all. In 1968 two of the largest railroads in the American Northeast—the Pennsylvania and the New York Central—created a company with gross trackage equal to that of the German Federal Republic and a book value in billions of dollars. But much of the trackage was useless, and the new company faced the future with almost no cash reserves. The two roads had been laid out to compete with each other; great savings were therefore expected from the merger as redundant lines were abandoned, duplicate facilities were merged, excess employees were dismissed, and efficiencies were achieved. But as it turned out, no employees could be dismissed and numbers of former employees actually had to be rehired, no serious financial provisions had been made to effect the merger, and the three principal officers of the combined corporation cordially detested each other. The two railroads were not merely competitive; they were designed to perform entirely different—and incompatible—functions.

Furthermore, although the Central's president, Alfred Perlman, was one of the boldest and most innovative railroad men of the century, he ran his company out of his hat and didn't employ modern financial methods; he became the new Penn Central's chief operations officer, responsible for a budget he did not understand. The Pennsy's financial controls were among the most modern and sophisticated in the country, but its operations were going to hell and its chief executive officer, Stuart Saunders, was a lawyer who possessed relatively little understanding of what was involved in running a giant transportation network; he became the Penn Central's chairman of the board. Between the two gentlemen stood a financial officer, David Bevan, who was widely respected on Wall Street and narrowly disliked in the executive suite; on merger day, he was stripped of much of his power to regulate the new corporation's money, which only he properly understood.

It wasn't so much a merger as a witches' brew, and two years later it resulted in the largest business failure in American history. It was also the last of the great traditional bankruptcies, as such events are understood in the usual economics textbooks—the Penn Central was basically a nineteenth-century company, badly managed and too generously financed, that went broke as a result of blunders—and as such, it was instructive, for it marked the beginning of an era when new ways of moving money around (rather than old ways of disposing of it) would place the economic life of the West at hazard.

Such merger plans as existed were preliminary and were never implemented. It was a catastrophe from the beginning. It wasn't merely that the Pennsylvania's computers couldn't talk to the New York Central's; the human management was likewise scarcely on speaking terms. The executive offices were in Philadelphia. The operations offices were in New York. Saunders, the chairman and chief executive officer, was more interested in using his railroad as a vehicle to found a conglomerate than he was in hauling freight; he belonged to all the best clubs in Philadelphia, a city of many fine clubs where running the old Pennsylvania railroad had been a gentleman's occupation. Bevan, the chief financial officer, was likewise a well-known clubman. Perlman, the chief operating officer, probably knew more about hauling freight than any other human being on the surface of the planet, but unlike Saunders and Bevan, he was a Jew and a railroad man. He stayed in New York and belonged to no Philadelphia clubs.

When Saunders was head of the Pennsy, he ran a company that was volume-oriented. Perlman's Central was profit-oriented—not at all the same thing. Saunders' hope was to batten on the assets of the Central until he could buy (among other things) an airline, which happened to be prohibited by government regulations. Perlman's purpose was to avoid being frozen out of the major realignment of the northeastern roads that was shaping up in the 1960s, an event at which the Central was proving to be somewhat of a wallflower. He then proposed to merge the yards, rationalize the trackage, modernize the equipment and the company structure, and make some money. Bevan's job was to raise enough cash to keep the company alive until either Saunders' philosophy triumphed, Perlman's did, or everything went smash. For this he needed some banks, and thereby hangs much of our tale.

Personalities, as always, play a great role in the fall of the Penn Central, but so does the use of other people's money. In an economy based on debt, a captain of industry and his lieutenants are no longer entirely masters of their corporate destiny—especially captains and lieutenants as hilariously mismatched as those at the railroad, with all the resultant possibilities for high corporate comedy. When a company depends for its survival on other people's money—say, in the form of the yield from the issues of commercial paper—it is at the mercy of market forces that are little understood outside the halls of finance, which may explain why corporate histories have lacked a certain zing they once possessed in the days of Ida Tarbell and her *History of the Standard Oil Company*.

But the reverse is also true: great debtors, like great rascals, tend to dominate their surroundings, and in the case of the Penn Central, a spacious portion of the immediate landscape was occupied by some large and powerful banks, which had loaned it a sum of money. When an individual or a company or a country borrows a large sum of money, as the Penn Central had, it becomes a valued customer, and when such a valued customer gets into the Penn Central's sort of trouble, its options are two. It can hope that its debt is so huge that its creditors will be forced to keep it alive in the anticipation of eventual repayment, or it can fiddle with its books and hope that the creditors won't notice. The story of the fall of the Penn Central is therefore as much the story of its loans as it is of the individual decisions of a handful of men. Love and money explain most things in this imperfect world, and in looking at the case of the Penn Central, the task is therefore an obvious one: follow the money.

First, some background. In the end, it was the Central that was serious about running its trains and the Pennsy that dreamed strange and wild dreams, but it was not always so. Ironically, throughout much of their separate existence, it was the Central that was the flash road, while the Pennsy had class. Founded in 1846 by a group of Philadelphia gentlemen investors determined to snatch back the commercial palm that had gone to Baltimore, with its National Road, and New York, with its Erie Canal, the Pennsylvania line operated under a peculiar constraint: that it should never embarrass the men who had put up the money. Under the leadership of such men as J. Edgar Thompson, the legendary engineer who laid out the main line so perfectly it has never been resurveyed, and Alexander J. Cassatt—remembered today as the brother of painter Mary Cassatt but known in his day as the visionary leader who drove the tracks into Manhattan and raised Penn Station to celebrate his triumph—the company was true to its trust. It was not only the best-managed line in the country, but it was also the most advanced—pioneering, for example, in electrification—and if Thompson had lived and gotten his way, it would have reached the Pacific. It is said that well-bred Philadelphia children were instructed to pray for three first things: the Republican party, the Girard Bank, and the Philadelphia Railroad. The railroad never missed a dividend. On the other hand, it didn't restore Philadelphia to commercial preeminence, either. Having seized the lead, the unruly New Yorkers kept it.

The Central was a very different kind of road. Established in 1853 through a merger of ten upstate lines and led by Albany plutocrat Erastus Corning (who is not, as whimsical fib has it, still serving as mayor of that city; it is one of his descendants who has occupied the office for almost longer than living men have memory), it originally terminated at Buffalo and on the Hudson. It was subsequently acquired by Commodore Vanderbilt in a famous raid. (First, he acquired control of the Hudson River Railroad, connecting Albany and New York, and then, in the middle of the winter of 1866–67, he refused to accept Central passengers and freight. By November 1867, his enemies were checkmated for the last time, and the line was his.)

The old Commodore bought the Central as a speculation, but, unlike other railroad speculators such as Jim Fisk, Jay Gould, Daniel Drew, and Henry "the Silent" Keep, he ran it like a business. At this distance, it is impossible to know what bug bit him so late in life, but it is safe to say that Cornelius Vanderbilt spent his last years as a genuine railroad man. He united his lines and brought them into New York. He built the first Grand Central, and his son William carried on the work, taking the road to Chicago and St. Louis and penetrating the territory of the secure and mighty Pennsylvania.

William's mergers were epochal, but he had the sense to realize that the days of the entrepreneur were passing. In 1883 he formally retired and handed the reins over to the lawyers and technicians who would dominate the golden age of railroading and ultimately preside over the long, slow atrophication of American capitalism. Still, he remained in the picture, not least because he had picked a war with the Pennsylvania by allying himself with Andrew Carnegie and had begun construction of the South Pennsylvania, a new line, straight into the heartland of his great rival's market. It was not until 1885 that Chauncey DePew (for the Central) and George Roberts (for the Pennsylvania) met on J. P. Morgan's yacht, the *Corsair,* and under the watchful eye of the financier patched up a truce that lasted the better part of a century. (Years later, the South Pennsylvania, its roadbeds and tunnels fallen into ruin, became part of the Pennsylvania Turnpike.)

Much is made by ideologues of the romance and advantages of cutthroat competition, which is often confused with capitalism. Indeed, as Morgan understood very well, competition and capitalism are often enemies and seldom friends. The purpose of capitalism is to create wealth—an endeavor that flourishes in peace—whereas competition is like war, destructive of capital and therefore wasteful and pointless. Like the elder Rockefeller but somewhat more consciously, Morgan realized that monopoly is therefore capitalism's most congenial way of doing business, and in overseeing the *Corsair* compact, a pair of monopolies was what he was attempting to create.

Having agreed upon a community of interest, the Central and the Pennsylvania settled down to enjoy the fruits of their separate labors, each in its own sector of the map. Hardly perfect monopolies, they still sought to attract business from each other, but it was more like a game than a battle and it had little to do with their corporate destinies, which resided elsewhere.

The Pennsy, with its lines to Pittsburgh and the coal country, became a volume road. Because of the terrain involved, the roadbed and equipment were harder to maintain, but the possibilities of bulk shipping more than made up for the handicaps of the landscape. The industry of its heartland required vast quantities of coal and raw materials, and one carload of coal is much like any other carload of coal. This simplifies railroad management wonderfully, since the management has to worry only about delivering specific quantities of simple commodities, omitting much bothersome paperwork; no matter where the coal or the ore came from to begin with, they eventually reached their destination in the desired quantity. The products of the foundries were similarly fungible, pig iron and steel girders being what they are, and their waybills were likewise simplified. As long as the road's freight remained pleasingly anonymous (iron ore, standardized girders), moving it about in the specified quantities was all that mattered, and as long as sufficient volume flowed over the rails, the company's profit more or less took care of itself.

The Central's water-level route was much less exciting, but it was also considerably cheaper to maintain. This advantage was more than offset, however, by the nature of the Central's market. Although the road hauled a certain amount of coal, the bulk of its business consisted of the finished products of a great variety of businesses and industries, which were scattered all over the map (along with their customers). Translated into colloquial terms, this meant that the Central's management, unlike the Pennsy's, was forced to hustle. Take, for example, a carload of bathtubs. Bathtubs come in a variety of makes and models, and the customer will require a very specific mix of the product. A carload will be picked up at the factory (along with a number of other, dissimilarly mixed cars) and conveyed to the yards, where it will be assigned to a specific train with a specific destination, along with cars loaded with other and very different products. The science of yard management was therefore considerably more precise at the Central than at the Pennsy.

The most economical train is, obviously, the longest one that can be pulled. At the Pennsy, this posed no particular problem; the dispatchers simply sent off thus-and-so many tons of coal to Pittsburgh, and that was it. On the Central, the trains had to be much more carefully composed, with the last cars the first to be dropped off at smaller yards along the route and from thence conveyed to the customers' sidings— and so on down the line, which is a good deal more exacting, a good deal more expensive, and a great deal more fragile an operation, especially when you consider that the customer not only demanded a specific product in a specific place, but he expected to receive it at a specific time.

To put it another way, the Pennsy might be considered a kind of controlled avalanche, whereas the Central was a fleet of taxicabs. In good years for the economy, the Central might do very well indeed, but a poor year could be a major set-back—a disaster unless the management retained its edge. And because the Central's cash flow and capital accumulation fluctuated considerably even under the best of circumstances, it was considerably more dependent on bank financing for operations, maintenance, and modernization than its plodding rival, eating further into profits. If the Central was to survive and prosper, it required the best management in the business, and even that might not be enough.

Thus the Pennsy and the Central—very different kinds of roads—started down the long slope of the twentieth century. The Federal Railroad Administration wore out their lines and their equipment during World War I. They had only partially recovered when the Depression struck; the Pennsy soldiered on in straitened circumstances, but by 1938, the Central was in deep trouble. World War II is widely thought to have been the railroads' last heyday—and, indeed, they performed splendidly—but the war once again took its toll on the road-beds and the aging rolling stock. In the immediate postwar years, the roads poured in more capital, accumulated and borrowed, to bring themselves back up to par even as the government spent profligately to create just the sort of suburbanized automobile culture in which very few eastern railroads could function profitably or, for that matter, at all.

Railroads require a certain demographic logic to survive: they function best when connecting concentrated nodes of humanity with other concentrated nodes of humanity, and during the postwar years, the government was doing its level best to scatter the population and its industry all over the landscape, while leaving the cities to the unproductive, nonconsuming poor. It likewise subsidized the airlines, and it subsidizes the airlines still. Meanwhile, the Interstate Commerce Commission (ICC) and many congressional liberals persisted in viewing the railroads as though they were still back in the days of the great railroad wars, with the Commodore, his son William, and their bottomless purses still in charge. Rises in rates were given grudgingly, if at all, and they were never enough. Uneconomical routes and unprofitable passenger traffic could not be abandoned—in large part because of social reasons that seemed perfectly valid at the time, however irrational they appear in retrospect. Hindsight is a wonderful thing; we know the story well, now that it has happened. When one adds to the social and demographic burdens the fact that the roads were paying massive taxes that their competitors in the airline and trucking industries were entirely free of, it is easy to see how the golden goose was led to slaughter. As a final insult, the government began to take away the mail and give it to the planes and trucks.

And yet, some way had to be found for the railroads to survive. The Northeast, the nation's workshop, was still dependent on them, and without them it would fail. But given the climate of opinion that prevailed in the fifties and sixties, it was clear that the railroads were going to have to arrange their survival for themselves. As it happened, the burden of the task fell squarely on the shoulders of a group of men as unlikely and ill-assorted as ever assembled outside a Hollywood army squad.

First, however, the industry was distracted by the spectacular arrival and equally spectacular departure of Robert Young. Speculators had changed since the old days. Vanderbilt, Drew, Keep, Fisk, and Gould had been nakedly and avariciously interested in money and didn't much care who knew it. Young, a Texan with powerful connections to du Pont, General Motors, and Cyrus Eaton, was a manipulator who made his fortune by selling short before the Crash of 1929, augmented it pleasingly during the Depression, yet nevertheless felt obliged to excuse his activities with the mask of anti-Wall Street populism. Although he knew next to nothing about running a railroad, either then or later, he became in the late 1930s very interested in the Chesapeake and Ohio and the Allegheny (the latter a railroad holding company founded by the improbable Van Swerigen brothers, who started out as real estate speculators in Shaker Heights, Ohio, decided to get into trolley lines, and ended up controlling $3 billion worth of railroads). Young was a genius at the manipulation of both stocks and public opinion, and he achieved control of the companies after a series of complicated maneuvers. Next, he stirred up a controversy over the Pullman Company's divestiture of its sleeping-car business, courting the public with visions of transcontinental travel with no change in Chicago, and he used the ensuing battle as an excuse to take over the Central. It took years and an enormous expenditure of cash and energy, but in 1954, he finally succeeded.

There is no doubt that he was entirely serious about a revival of the great days of passenger travel, by the way. For once, however, his romantic self-image as a populist from Wall Street got the better of his common sense. With the equipment aging, the lines in decline, and the federal government lavishly subsidizing automobiles and planes, private rail passenger service was doomed; even as Young moved in on the Central, the Eisenhower administration was gearing up for the most massive highway program in the nation's history.

But if Young was a romantic, he was no fool. He had merely controlled the C&O and the Allegheny group, not run them, and he realized that the Central was going to need superlative management if it was to survive and, perhaps, prosper again. To this end he brought in a new president, Alfred Perlman, a graduate of MIT and Harvard, who as a student had assisted in the rebuilding of the Burlington and as a young man had brought the Denver and Rio Grand Western (D&RGW) back from the brink of bankruptcy. Perlman was an advocate of automation, personnel cuts, and drastic rebuilding, and he had no use for passenger trains whatever.

In 1954, the Central was in a bad way, overstaffed, underutilized, and with a poor capital position. To make matters worse, the Eisenhower administration was not only committed to massive highway building, it was also committed to the Saint Lawrence Seaway, which would destroy the Central's midwestern export business. Perlman's strategy was twofold: to make the line as lean and efficient as possible, and to find a merger partner, preferably a high-volume line hauling commodities that couldn't be transferred to trucks and ships. First, however, he had to save the line and place it in a position of strength.

He let the commuter lines go to hell. He fired 25,000 employees. He cut the maintenance budget to the marrow, and he abandoned as many unprofitable and marginal services as the ICC would allow. The Central was not only a railroad, it was a real estate company that owned a sizable hunk of midtown Manhattan, including the Commodore and Biltmore hotels and the Yale Club. Perlman sold off some of the properties and improved others; the hotels' profit shot up by 50 percent. Like other railroads, the Central had investments in other transportation companies; Perlman dipped into the portfolio and distributed shares of the Reading and U.S. Freight in lieu of stockholder dividends. Moreover, the Eisenhower boom was on—the last genuine boom the country was to see in decades—and the Central, properly handled, always did very well in prosperous times. The line reported earnings of $8.78 a share in 1955 and $6.58 in 1956. With these figures in hand, Perlman was able to reenter the capital markets, raising money for new freight cars and diesel locomotives. He ran fewer trains, longer trains, and more modern trains, and he began to build new yards. His marketing department became one of the finest in the country. But although he argued eloquently and prophetically, he was forbidden to abandon his marginal passenger lines, and the New York Thruway had begun to take away his business. The company was also being taxed to death, and its taxes were going to its competitors.

With all his ruthless brilliance and ingenuity, Perlman had given the Central some space to breathe but only that, and it had been achieved at the expense of Robert Young's dreams. There was no hope for the passenger business, and Young's resuscitated freight business continued to be more susceptible to the fluctuations of the business cycle than were his volume-oriented competitors. He had hoped to award his stockholders with consistently generous dividends, but he couldn't. Robert Young had always been subject to crippling bouts of depression. On January 25, 1958, he shot himself.

The years 1957 and 1958 were recession years. Railroad earnings were hard hit, and the highway program was accelerated to ease unemployment. Led by Perlman, the railroads asked Washington for relief, but little was forthcoming; like armies, governments are more comfortable fighting the wars of the past than those of the present and the future, and neither the administration nor the Congress seemed capable of understanding what was going on. As far as the railroads were concerned, the handwriting was on the wall. It was time to take a step that had been long deferred. It was time to effect the great mergers that had been talked of since the early years of the century and hope that it was not too late.

The Erie was the first. The weakest of the great eastern roads, it had never recovered from the manipulations of Daniel Drew a hundred years before. None of the other majors wanted it and it finally ended up combining with the Delaware, Lackawanna, and Western, but it was more a death watch than a merger. The Norfolk and Western, a prosperous coal-hauling road of great strength, improved its position by absorbing the Virginian Railroad and wisely looked no further. The Baltimore and Ohio—like the Central, a flash road with a heavy burden of debt—sought a natural partner with the C&O, another coal line with a small overburden of passengers, and a merger was eventually effected. That left the Pennsy and the Central, but in the end, it was less a merger than a raid.

While Perlman and his whiz kids were putting the Central back together, the Pennsy was on the skids. The freight business was still profitable—in 1953 it brought in a gross of $787 million, or more than the combined totals of the B&O and C&O—but because it connected the Northeast's largest cities, the Pennsy had also evolved into the nation's largest passenger line. The business could be pared a little but it couldn't be abandoned—the Interstate Commerce Commission wouldn't allow that, and the deficits were chronic; in 1957, the passenger division lost $57 million. As recently as 1951, however, the deficit had been $72 million. There are indications that if the road had been able to attract someone like Perlman (and had gotten him interested in hauling people rather than freight), something might have been done, but the Pennsy's management was traditionally stolid rather than bold, and the company was poorly organized. The old corporate structure established by Edgar Thompson for his westward push no longer worked very well, and the well-bred management lacked nerve and vision. The company that had once been a money machine was now heavily in debt, and the hole was getting deeper. In 1958, the Pennsy reported earnings of $3.5 million and would have registered a loss without $18 million in retroactive mail pay from the government. The Pennsy's executive suite was the home of gentlemen, but they were not deep thinkers and only one solution to the dilemma seemed to occur to them: merge with the rejuvenated Central, even if it meant the company would have to swallow Perlman as part of the deal.

It never seemed to have occurred to anyone at the railroad that Perlman might, in fact, be the instrument of their salvation; and with the appointment of Stuart Saunders to the chairmanship, the point became moot. It developed that Saunders, a lawyer by training and a lobbyist by inclination, wasn't solely interested in running a railroad. What he had in mind instead was running a conglomerate.

Later, while the dust from the collapse still hung thickly in the air, Perlman would make much of the fact that it wasn't a merger but a takeover, that the Central had been captured by the Pennsy and then destroyed. At a high point in the company's fortunes, he had gone so far as to say that the Central had become a recession-proof railroad, and he later testified that he thought the Central could have made it on its own. True, Perlman had made the Central as efficient and cost-effective as was humanly possible, but he was still faced with the menace of the highways and the Seaway, the passenger business refused to go away, the other roads were moving toward combination, and he was being forced into a narrower and narrower corner.

For a while, Perlman and Young thought that a union with the C&O might be an answer. Miles of competitive track could be eliminated, duplicate facilities could be scrapped, and they and their marketing department believed—probably correctly—that they could do wonders there. Unfortunately, the problems that would have to be overcome—not least, the Central's persistent lack of capital—proved insurmountable and a great chance was lost. That left the Pennsylvania merger or nothing; nothing else was possible.

The initiative came from Philadelphia, specifically from James Miller Symes, the baggage master's son who had risen through the ranks to the very head of the railroad. Like Perlman, Symes could count. Unlike Perlman, he was not uneasy in his mind. As far as he was concerned, a merger of the

Pennsylvania and the Central was as natural as bacon and eggs. With his board's permission, he met with Young in New York in September 1957 and later with Young and Perlman at White Sulphur Springs, West Virginia. A joint announcement that the merger was under study was issued in November.

After Young's suicide and Perlman's ascension to supreme command, the Central's ardor cooled notably; Perlman still wanted the C&O and he thought the Pennsy's natural partner was the Norfolk and Western (which it partly owned). Formal talks were broken off in January 1959, but not before a committee report had been issued estimating merger savings at $80 million—a magic number, arrived at somewhat mysteriously, that was to become something of an idée fixe on the part of the Pennsy's management. Somehow, no one knew quite how, an $80 million dividend was to fall into their laps and the fat thus pulled from the fire. It was an article of faith—but not, it should be noted, to Alfred Perlman.

Perlman went haring off after the C&O. He failed to obtain it, and in 1961 he was back where Symes wanted him, at the Pennsy's negotiating table. In the deal that was eventually cobbled together, the Pennsy would absorb the Central, with the Central's stockholders receiving 40 percent of the new entity. The board would consist of fourteen Pennsylvania directors and eleven Central. How the combined roads were to arrange their management and operations was left for later, and the problem of the Pennsy's mounting debt was mentioned only by David Bevan, the Pennsy's financial wizard. On the evidence, no one paid much attention to him, least of all Stuart Saunders, who succeeded Symes as chairman of the PRR in late 1963 as the merger was slowly making its way through hearings before the ICC.

Although Saunders had headed the Norfolk and Western at the time of its successful merger with the Virginian, his talents lay elsewhere. With its lock on the West Virginia coal fields, its minimal passenger service, its fine roadbed and equipment, and its comfortable debt position, the N&W more or less ran itself. Saunders' chief asset, aside from his sunny optimism and his considerable social grace, was his formidable political skill, conspicuously but not exclusively represented by his friendship with Lyndon Baines Johnson.

The very day that Saunders assumed command of the Pennsy, the Kennedy administration expressed disapproval of the merger. Saunders immediately set out to earn his salary; indeed, if Stuart Saunders can be said to have had a finest hour, this was it. Following a combined Pennsy–Central lobbying blitz that has been described as "little short of sensational," Governor William Scranton reversed his predecessor's position and brought the state of Pennsylvania conditionally into line behind the merger; New Jersey followed. Lyndon Johnson was in the White House by then, and the new administration's attitude was dramatically different. David Lawrence, the four-time mayor of Pittsburgh who as governor had opposed the combined road, chaired the President's Committee on Equal Opportunity in Housing; abruptly, he experienced second thoughts on the matter, and his conversion was accompanied by action. Despite Governor Scranton's approval, numbers of towns around the state still opposed the merger. Lawrence exerted persuasive force, appealing to the loyalty of the local Democrats and to the economic preoccupations of the local Republicans. He also made it clear that certain federal subsidies might no longer be forthcoming if his agency began investigations in communities that remained recalcitrant.

In 1966, the ICC approved the merger, and new light was seen by the Justice Department. "Johnson brought the Democratic National Committee to work for Saunders," said Milton Shapp, himself a Democrat who ran for governor of Pennsylvania that year on a platform that vigorously opposed the merger. Shapp found himself checkmated at every turn. He also found himself attacked in the press. At the time, the owner of the Philadelphia *Inquirer* was Walter Annenberg, who was simultaneously the largest noninstitutional stockholder in the Pennsylvania Railroad. The *Inquirer* printed stories linking Shapp to a criminal and a white supremacist, men who had in fact been dismissed from his campaign when their affiliations became known. An *Inquirer* reporter asked the candidate if he had ever been in a mental institution. The paper headlined his startled denial the next day. Shapp lost the election.

Annenberg was apparently acting on his own, but Saunders was not idle. While winning the day in Washington and witnessing the miraculous conversion of ex-Governor Lawrence, he defused any potential opposition from organized labor by negotiating the Merger Protection Agreement of 1964, in which he virtually gave away the farm. Normally, when a railroad merger was effected, employees were protected in their jobs for four years. Saunders offered lifetime protection. He also agreed to rehire any of the five thousand employees who were dismissed between the time of the merger agreement and the merger itself (about twenty-four hundred presumably overjoyed employees availed themselves of the offer), and he tacked on a year's severance pay for anyone who was fired. The opposition of the unions miraculously evaporated.

One doesn't have to go far to discover the source of Saunders' astonishing generosity. He had some interesting plans. In these plans, the railroad figured prominently as a vehicle, but not solely one for carrying objects on steel wheels and steel tracks. Instead, Saunders seems to have seen himself as a modern buccaneer, like Charles Bluhdorn or James Ling, and his railroad as a means to achieve a conglomerate—the great fata morgana of the go-go sixties, in pursuit of which so many careers were wrecked.

The idea of a conglomerate is basically a very simple one, and it is this: fish that have money eat fish that don't. Back in the bad old days of the robber barons, entrepreneurs would attempt to achieve something called vertical integration, controlling all aspects of their product's manufacture from its cradle as a raw material to its grave in the hands of the customer, who would consume it. One therefore found steel companies that owned iron and coal mines, the means of transporting ore to and steel from the mills, and companies that shaped the girders into buildings and bridges. The dangers of price manipulation were obvious; a vertically integrated company could gouge its competition by charging itself preferential rates, and once the competition was destroyed, it could gouge the customers by reversing the process with arbitrary price hikes. But economic processes were somewhat better understood in those days and a number of commendable laws were passed to prevent the practice. Companies also branched out into horizontal integration, whereby a railroad would turn itself into a transportation company by buying trucking lines (as both the Pennsy and the Central did), bus companies, and passenger airlines (as the Pennsy partially did, when it acquired an interest in Greyhound and the predecessor of TWA). The benefits of horizontal integration were obvious, the dangers were not quite so clear, and legislative remedies were applied piecemeal, if at all; for example, railroads were forbidden to own airlines, but the Penn Central was able to carry its trucking companies with it into bankruptcy.

A conglomerate, by contrast, is a horse designed by a committee. The only reason a company was attached to a conglomerate was because it was profitable, or potentially so; it didn't matter what it manufactured, or what service it performed, just so long as it made money and could be obtained. An unsurprised world was treated to the spectacle of companies that made automotive parts and owned armored cars, companies that traded in land and made movies, companies that made airplanes and submarines. These are only some of the more rational examples; a conglomerate could, theoretically and in practice, combine any sort of incompatible entities.

Vertical and horizontal integration are sound attempts to rationalize an industry for the purpose of maximizing profits;

a conglomerate is simply a series of acquisitions assembled solely for the purpose of making a buck and usually based on a single company with a long line of credit. This leads to some problems. For one thing, it is somewhat unlikely that the officers of the parent company will have the faintest notion of how to run, say, their baby food, gas mask, and pantyhose subsidiaries, with the result that the subsidiaries will either stagnate or go wild in the absence of intelligent supervision from the center. Even more likely, since the purpose of a conglomerate is the making of money rather than the imposition of order, is that the officers of the parent company will put the profits and credit of those subsidiaries to some highly creative, even questionable, uses; and in the case of the Penn Central, that is exactly what happened.

Symes had already begun a program to develop the road's real estate, laying plans to demolish Penn Station in New York and Broad Street Station in Philadelphia, and to sell the air rights over the Chicago facilities to real estate speculators, taking advantage of a law designed to protect architectural landmarks by allowing them to auction off the empty space above their rooflines to construction tycoons, who then use them to circumvent the zoning ordinances. Saunders stepped up the pace. Using the Pennsylvania Company, a nearly moribund subsidiary originally set up by Edgar Thompson to acquire western lines, he acquired the Buckeye Pipeline Company and three real estate operations: Great Southwestern, Arvida, and Macco. We shall be hearing more about these shortly. He also made moves to acquire an airline. It is illegal for a railroad to own an airline.

Meanwhile, the merger inched forward. The Interstate Commerce Commission examiners recommended it in March 1965, and the commissioners issued their formal approval more than a year later, on April 27, 1966. The Justice Department dropped its opposition in November 1967. Various lawsuits held the matter up until January 1968, when the Supreme Court gave its formal blessing, and on February 1, with Perlman at pains to cast himself in the role of disgruntled spectator—like Achilles sulking in his tent, he refused to emerge from his private car to witness the unveiling of the new corporate logo—the companies were combined. It was the largest merger in American corporate history. It survived—if that is the word for it—for 872 days.

On paper it looked good. The new company commanded 20,570.29 miles of track, 94,453 employees, 186 different companies, $6.2 billion in assets, and consolidated 1967 revenues of $2 billion. It was shortly to grow even larger, due to the ICC's insistence that it also absorb the New Haven—and, of course, the New Haven's $22 million annual loss. On paper, this seemed a marvel of simplicity: the Transportation Company owned the Pennsylvania Company, and the Pennsylvania Company owned the new subsidiaries. It was, in short, a sleek giant of American enterprise, with vast resources at its command and a captive market at its doorstep. It was time to start saving that $80 million.

Everything immediately went to hell, and it never got better again.

In the merging of two great enterprises, there are two schools of thought: the slow and the fast. Under the slow method, the companies continue to function as separate entities while their operations are subtly and carefully combined over a period of months and years. This means that the savings expected from the merger are equally slow in coming, but the separate teams learn to work together, the bookkeeping gets reconciled, and any problems can be handled piecemeal. The difficulty is that it takes lots and lots of time. The fast method takes much less time, and the resultant savings are, presumably, placed on the corporate table much earlier. It is not, however, as simple as a magician clapping a pair of cymbals together and producing a pigeon, although the relevant Pennsylvania and Central executives—including Alfred Perlman, who henceforth behaved like a man with a corporate death wish—acted as though it were.

A rapid merger requires complicated and finely tuned preliminary planning. To this end, the roads drew up a document called the Patchell study, which was hastily drawn and presented to the ICC as the actual merger plan. The Patchell study had very little to do with reality, although it sounded good, and it was never heard of again.

In any merger, it is important for the officers of the combining companies to know what they will be doing after the merger is effected; it helps them to plan their future. Somehow this simple fact—along with many other equally simple facts—seems to have escaped the attention of those involved. Only Saunders and Perlman had any idea of what they would be doing after merger day. Saunders was to be chairman of the board and chief executive officer. He was to remain in Philadelphia, and so would the offices of the Pennsylvania Company, the instrument Saunders had chosen to create his nonrailroad conglomerate. Perlman was to be president and chief operating officer, heading up the offices of the Transportation Company (which, as was mentioned before, officially owned the Pennsylvania Company) in New York. While the geographical and organizational structure thus created was clumsy and fraught with peril, it presumably suited both men, who didn't like each other. Moreover, neither of them liked David Bevan, the Pennsy's brilliant but egocentric financial officer, who wound up as chairman of the new Penn Central finance committee but who was dropped as a member of the board of directors, something that didn't make him happy and that complicated his life enormously, since the other six members of the committee were on the board. Bevan's powers were further limited by the fact that, for some reason, Perlman controlled budget administration, data processing, accounting, taxes, and insurance, and seemed determined to run the railroad out of his hat.

At the Pennsy, Bevan had introduced the most modern

accounting practices, including income and expense budgets that accounted for the movement and placement of every penny the railroad had. At the Central, Perlman had used an antiquated method of accounting that enabled him to run the company, in effect, on a day-to-day basis out of the corporate checkbook, managing the company's affairs as though it were a family and Perlman its daddy. Doubtless the method was more congenial to his aggressive temperament, and perhaps it didn't matter what kind of accounting was employed as long as somebody knew how much money there was. Now Bevan had some functions and Perlman had others, and on merger day Perlman threw Bevan's modern methods out the window. He set out to rescue the Penn Central with the energy of despair. But he was trying to do so on a road that was immediately plunged into anarchy by the merger, and he no longer had any idea of how many coins were in the corporate till. Bevan had a somewhat better idea, but Perlman wouldn't listen to him, while Saunders—the author of all this financial mischief when he stripped vital functions away from his chief financial officer—wouldn't help.

In merging any two companies—especially in merging them rapidly—it is vitally important that some very delicate adjustments be made in the areas of finance, marketing, and operations, as these will be the heart of the new corporation. Not only was Bevan given no idea what he would be doing after the merger (when, as we have seen, he resurfaced with severely limited powers) but neither he nor his opposite number at the Central was predisposed to cooperate with the other, and they didn't. Minimal planning was done, and the computer departments were at loggerheads.

Cooperation was better in the marketing departments, but the question of whether the new road would be volume-oriented (like the Pennsy) or profit-oriented (like the Central) was not resolved, in no small part because the Central's superb marketing officers viewed their Pennsylvania counterparts with distinct skepticism. In the upshot, the conflict was resolved by default in the immediate postmerger period, because most of the Central people left the company.

In the operations departments the Patchell report was scrapped once it had served the purpose of persuading the ICC, and a joint committee labored for two and a half years to draw up a master plan. It eventually ran to six volumes, but its recommendations were too time-consuming to satisfy Perlman. In November 1967, less than three months before merger day, he ordered it stamped "Preliminary" and effectively scrapped it. On February 1, 1968, there was no operating plan.

The two largest railroads in the United States were about to merge, and nobody knew what to do. The chief officers of the new company detested each other. Many of their subordinates were hardly on speaking terms. It was an astonishing situation.

There was immediate chaos all along the lines. The two roads weren't nearly as compatible as the ICC had been led to believe. The old Central yards weren't large enough to handle the combined new business and neither were the Pennsy's. Because none of the dispatchers was adequately retrained and the new system was sketchy, massive congestion developed at such major choke points as Chicago and Cleveland, where there were duplicate yards. Waybills were lost. So were individual shipments and even whole trains. Dispatchers began sending out trains just to get rid of them. Car revenues declined. Per diem rates—the amount the railroad paid for the use of cars from other systems—shot through the ceiling. Shippers abandoned the road in droves. "We started mixing up people, and the problems were inevitable," said one Penn Central executive. "All of a sudden dispatchers were getting orders to run trains to West Jockstrap."

Meanwhile, in a misguided effort to accelerate a merger that was racing hellbent toward disaster, new procedures were promulgated before the procedures they supplanted were understood. Perlman did what he could—by the end of 1969, he had managed to consolidate the terminals in thirty-five cities, but at a suicidal cost of $121 million. He replaced his two chief subordinates—former Pennsy men—with former Central executives, which improved efficiency but aggravated the tensions within the company. Things slowly seemed to get better, but the improvement was more apparent than real. In 1968, the road spent 83.62 cents on operations for every dollar that was taken in. In 1969, the figure rose to 85.60 cents, fully 10 cents on the dollar greater than the line's competitors. Interest payments ran to $260,000 a day; passenger losses were $275,000 a day. The New Haven joined the system on January 1, 1969, and added its $22 million in annual losses and another $22 million that it took to upgrade its equipment. At the time of the merger, it was projected that the Merger Protection Agreement would cost the line $78.2 million over eight years. In 1968 and 1969, it cost $64.7 million; in 1970 it cost another $28 million. There was no realistic way to cut back on the number of employees without paying around $12,000 to each one who was dismissed. As late as 1970, somewhere between 277 and 351 Penn Central boxcars somehow found their way to the LaSalle and Bureau County Railroad, where they were repainted and rented back to the company that owned them. To Bevan's despair, Perlman continued to operate without an income budget, and yet he was asking for $1.5 billion to run the railroad during the single year of 1968.

Income budget or not, Perlman's $1.5 billion was probably close to the mark if the railroad was to be saved; it may even have been modest. He was going about his job in the only way that might have worked: ripping the road apart and putting it back together again, just as he'd done at the D&RGW and the Central. At the D&RGW and the Central, however, he had been dealing with a pair of relatively tractable emergencies. At the Penn Central, he was confronted with calamity. Some of the problems were obvious—the operational chaos caused by the merger, the takeover of marketing by former Pennsy men, the burden of Saunders' Merger Pro-

tection Agreement, and the ICC's perennial lack of realism.
(In 1969, the road's labor costs went up 9 percent; the ICC
granted an interim rise of 3 percent in June and finally got
around to granting 5 percent in November, which is a little
like throwing a drowning man half a rope after hours of sol-
emn consideration.) Still, Perlman might eventually have begun to make some headway if it hadn't been for another small
problem.

The Penn Central didn't have $1.5 billion. It didn't have
anything like the amount of money it told its stockholders, the
investment community, and the press that it had. The company was "cooking" the books to make them reflect profitable
cash flows that did not exist. It has never been clear whether
or not Perlman was aware of the fact—such evidence as exists
suggests that he probably wasn't—but the question was
shortly rendered moot. Desperate to cut expenses, Saunders
maneuvered Perlman out of the presidency and into the
powerless position of vice chairman of the board. On December 1, 1969, Paul Gorman, former head of Western Electric
and a man who had no experience at running a railroad, was
installed as his successor. The Penn Central's last slim hope
was gone, but Saunders hardly seemed to notice. He still
seemed to hope that the railroad could somehow be forced to
make money. Then it began to snow.

It was the snow that did the Penn Central in, finally, a
natural phenomenon that occurs, with greater or lesser severity, every year in the vicinity of December. Much was made
of this amazing event, as though God had just invented something new. Switches froze, trains ground to a halt, and the
company carried on as though it had spent the last hundred
and a quarter years in Brazil. There was no longer any way to
conceal the extent of the operating disaster, and the resultant
losses also revealed that the line was out of cash. In truth, the
storm only made clear something that had been artfully con-
cealed by some highly creative bookkeeping: the merger had

destroyed both lines, the Pennsy was dragging the Central down with it, and the money well was utterly dry.

The Penn Central's collapse under the weight of a blanket of precipitation came as an enormous surprise to a great many people who had been living with the carefully fostered delusion that they were looking at a profitable company. In 1968, the first year of the merger, the Penn Central reported consolidated earnings of $87,689,000, and Saunders and Perlman issued a glowing report to their stockholders. True, service had gone to hell in a handcart and the railroad division had posted a loss of $5,155,000, but the company had a $275 million merger reserve to cover such expected contingencies and the diversification program was clearly paying handsome dividends. The next year, 1969, the reported profit shrank to $4,388,000, while the railroad division reported a whopping $56,328,000 loss, a tenfold increase in a single year. This was bad, but it hardly seemed crucial. Dividends were paid—$55,400,000 in 1968, $43,396,000 in 1969, when the fourth-quarter payment was omitted. At worst, the company might be viewed as troubled but hardly a candidate for collapse; in addition to the profitable new subsidiaries, there were its extensive real estate holdings, and it seemed that the company, in extremity, could live for a long time by cannibalizing its assets.

In actual fact, the real estate holdings were mortgaged to the hilt, to the extent that it was impossible to raise long-term bank money, and the company was subsisting on short-term credit and the sale of commercial paper. Short-term credit is a perfectly splendid thing to have if a company enjoys a decent cash flow, substantial reserves, and an established line of long-term bank funding. Under such circumstances, short-term credit gives the borrowing company the sort of flexibility—an ability to move swiftly and seize the main chance—a well-run enterprise requires, and there is no great risk involved. But when short-term credit is used as a substitute for long-term credit—to finance major capital projects, or to keep

a faltering enterprise alive until its executives think of something—it becomes dangerously unstable, especially if the company (as is likely) has very little money of its own.

It is axiomatic that when someone borrows money, he is
at the mercy of his bankers, but long-term credit is a sword
with two edges. If a company's (or a country's) books are fat
with long-term loans, loans that are to be paid back over a
period of years, the lenders develop a vested interest in that
company's (or that country's) continued health and well-
being, and at moments of crisis, it is much easier to raise additional cash, since the lenders are understandably eager to protect their long-term involvement. (As we shall see, Brazil and
others of the richer less-developed countries were able to
raise vast sums in just this way, following the oil shocks of
1973 and 1979. General Motors and Ford were likewise able
to tide themselves over the liquidity crisis of 1980.)

But short-term loans are loans whose life is measured in
months, and they are not automatically renewable; each fresh
short-term loan must be negotiated anew. If a company is living off short-term cash, taking brief loans as the old brief
loans expire (another term for this is rollover), it is wise to
keep its creditors happy and unsuspicious, or the day will very
shortly come when it will go too often to the well, with a pile
of bills to pay and no money to do so. Corporate death invariably follows. Rollovers are seldom a very good idea at the
best of times, although circumstances in the capital markets
may require them, but a company that resorts to the tactic
ought to be sure it is in the pink of health, and it ought to
have substantial reserves in the form of quantities of unencumbered cash.

The new Penn Central was neither very healthy nor did it
have a great deal of money of its own. Cash on hand on
merger day was $13.3 million, $7.8 million of which was
contributed by the hapless Central. This situation didn't get
better, it got worse. Moreover, the profits from the

diversification program and other subsidiaries were largely illusory.

Saunders' willingness to juggle the books—euphemistically called "earnings maximization"—went back at least to the premerger year of 1967, when he tried to conceal certain unpleasant deficits by lumping them together in the fourth quarter and, when the fourth quarter failed to prove profitable enough, to wait and hide them in the merger itself, when the Central's cash would act as a handy device for concealment. Members of the accounting department, more than a little concerned about going to jail, refused to play along, but Saunders' predisposition was clearly there—he was the chairman of the board, and he soon had his way in other matters.

Buckeye Pipeline was the crown jewel of Saunders' mini-conglomerate; it actually yielded some profits, although not enough to offset the railroad's investment in it. Using the Pennsylvania Company (Pennco for short), the railroad had acquired control of Buckeye between 1963 and 1965, at a total cost of $30,381,000, part of which was in the form of preferred Pennco stock. Since Pennco, like the railroad, paid dividends in the teeth of sound business practice, Buckeye received $19,488,000, through 1970. The shrewd observer will notice that the railroad was now out a total of $49,869,000, a tidy sum for a company with chronic and growing cash problems. In return, Buckeye paid Pennco dividends of $37,331,000, for a net deficit of $12,538,000.

There is thus far nothing particularly wrong with any of this, stupid though it may have been. Cooking the books is another matter. In 1968 and 1969, Buckeye's earnings came to $26,034,000, of which the railroad received $12,600,000 in the form of dividends. Nevertheless, the railroad's accounting department, pursuing Saunders' policy of income maximization, reported the entire sum as earnings, which looked good on paper, but which meant that the railroad was laying claim to around $13 million it didn't have—"Chinese money," in the words of one director who was gifted with an unusual amount of hindsight.

But the miracles were not over yet. Indeed, they had just begun. Like an optimist facing a firing squad, Saunders continued to attempt to strike bargains with fate. He kept after the accounting department, hoping it could find ways to avoid charging expenses against income. He tried to get the per diem charges adjusted downward. He raided the merger reserve—not an actual sum of money, but a bookkeeping device—in a way that produced no money but that seemed to keep costs down. He abandoned trackage and facilities without reflecting it on the books, because their cost (less scrap value) would have had to be charged to ordinary income. He wrote off $126 million worth of long-haul passenger facilities, despite the fact that they were still in use, and reported it to the stockholders (but not to the ICC, which wouldn't allow it) as an extraordinary item and thus not chargeable against ordinary income, achieving major but illusory savings in depreciation. He concealed (but, again, not from the ICC) $22 million worth of maintenance on the New Haven by disguising it as a rehabilitation cost not chargeable to ordinary income, which meant that the income reported to the stockholders was $22 million higher than the income reported to the ICC. The Penn Central Railroad owned 97.3 percent of the Lehigh Valley Railroad. In 1968 and 1969, the Lehigh Valley lost between $5 and $6 million a year. The loss was simply omitted from the consolidated balance sheet.

Although it drained cash away from the railroad, Buckeye Pipeline was easily the best investment Pennco ever made; given time, it might even have made the road some money. It was also compatible with the ostensible purpose of the Penn Central—it transported something—but in the years before the merger Stuart Saunders saw the future in a somewhat different way. The old Pennsy might be falling apart, but it owned a lot of real estate. On merger day it would acquire a good deal more, in the form of the Manhattan hotels Perlman had obligingly refurbished. Real estate was clearly the way to go.

In 1965, following a careful inspection of the property by Saunders and Bevan, Pennco bought the Macco Corporation, a southern California land company that also did business as a builder of single-family homes. The price was $39 million. Macco immediately went into a tailspin. By 1967, it required cash infusions of over $7 million a year.

The previous year, Pennco had acquired over 50 percent of the Great Southwest Corporation, a Texas land developer founded by the Wynne family and the Rockefellers. Further stock acquisitions brought Pennco's share up to 90 percent in 1969, and the ailing Macco was merged into Great Southwest. The total cost of the two entities (less the $7 million a year paid out to Macco) came to $87,365,000. In return, Great Southwest sent the railroad $4,256,000 in dividends, leaving the railroad with a staggering cash drain of $83,109,000.

Like Buckeye, Great Southwest and Macco had their uses. In December 1968, Macco sold its Bryant Ranch property to four hundred tax shelter–seeking investors for $31 million, resulting in a paper profit of $9,925,780. The investors paid $6,039,000 in cash, $600,000 as a down payment on the principal and the balance in prepaid, tax-deductible interest. No further principal payments were due until 1984. Interest payments at the 7 percent on the face of the note should have been $2,128,000 a year, but only $1 million a year (likewise tax-deductible) was required, with the balance coming due, again, after 1984. Moreover, under California law the investors were personally liable for nothing but their initial down payment in the event that they changed their minds, went broke, died, or took a powder. On its part, Macco was obliged to make recreational improvements to the tune of $5.5 million, develop lots for the investors, build a $4 million highway, and develop the property, 15 percent of which remained unsold.

Meanwhile Great Southwest was engaged in a similar

pair of sweetheart deals. The company owned two amusement parks, Six Flags over Texas and Six Flags over Georgia. The Georgia park was sold in December 1968 for $22,980,157. The investors fronted $2.95 million, of which $1.5 million was applied to principal and $1.45 million was prepaid interest. Subsequent interest payments were to run at $1,249,500 a year until 1974 and $759,000 thereafter until 2004. Principal payments of $700,000 were not to begin until 1974. The Texas park was sold in June 1969 for $40 million. The math is equally fascinating. The principal payment was $1.5 million and the prepaid interest was $3,932,670. Subsequent annual interest payments were $1,221,354 and principal payments were $1,094,331.

On close examination, it turns out that what Great Southwest had actually done was to sell off some tax breaks. The investors bought into a limited partnership. This entity then gave the parks to a second limited partnership, whose general partner was a subsidiary of Great Southwest, which continued to run them as though nothing had happened. The investors got their tax break, Great Southwest got a little front money, and Pennco got an enormous paper profit. Saunders was able to point to the wonders wrought by his diversification program, the value of Great Southwest's stock shot up, and Pennco, the 90-percent owner, was able to use it as collateral on some badly needed loans. That the money did not, in fact, exist was immaterial.

Pennco also owned 56 percent of the Arvida Corporation, a land company based in Florida. The investment cost $22,047,000. Arvida never paid a dividend. It nevertheless reported earnings of $3,749,000 in 1968 and 1969, and the railroad's $2.1 million share duly found its way into the books.

The Central contributed the Strick Holding Company, a truck trailer outfit, for which it paid $15 million. The Penn Central poured an additional $9,437,000 into the company before finally selling it for $15 million in 1968.

*   *   *

If these investments sound questionable, insane, or both, they aren't a patch on Executive Jet Aviation. In the teeth of reason, Saunders had convinced himself that the airlines were about to steal the freight business with giant aircraft like the C5A, just as the 707 had taken the passengers. Executive Jet Aviation, however, appears to have been Bevan's baby from the beginning. It was a beguiling idea, at least at first, before the hallucinatory quality that marked so many of the railroad's investments set in. EJA was an air taxi service for executives, similar to one its founder, Olbert F. Lassiter, had run for his colleagues when he was a brigadier general in the Air Force. Rather than going to the expense and trouble of maintaining its own aircraft, a company could simply whistle up a plane from EJA. Lassiter's board was impressive, too; it included Curtis LeMay, Jimmy Stewart, and Arthur Godfrey. All it needed was a little capital, and, as though obeying a perverse law of nature, it soon found itself gravitating in the direction of the great lumbering sugar daddy of corporate America, the Penn Central, thanks to the good offices of Bevan's friend and fellow speculator, General Charles Hodge of the brokerage firm Glore Forgan, who effected the necessary introductions.

Using the railroad's subsidiary American Contract Corporation, Bevan bought 56 percent of EJA, or 655,960 shares, for $327,980. By Penn Central standards, this was a mere drop in the bucket, but Bevan proceeded to live up to the railroad's reputation by pouring in more than $21 million worth of loans between 1965 and 1969 ($21,019,877, according to the Securities and Exchange Commission; $21,011,877.31, according to the House Committee on Banking and Currency), much of which sum went to subsidize General Lassiter's sybaritic life-style.

Bevan was pursuing a delicious mirage. Lassiter was negotiating to take control of the Johnson Flying Service of Missoula, Montana, which had been certified by the Civil Aeronautics Board (CAB) as a supplemental airline. The certificate would enable EJA to go into business in a big way. Not incidentally, it would also place the Penn Central in clear violation of the Federal Aviation Act of 1958, which quite specifically forbids the ownership of airlines by railroads. The PCR was clearly a railroad (despite Saunders' attempts to pretend it .was something else); EJA would definitely become an air carrier; and the PCR controlled EJA. In 1966, as the CAB began an investigation that could have only one conclusion, Lassiter bought two 707s and two 727s and signed a letter of intent to purchase six Lockheed L-500s, the civilian version of the C5A.

In 1967, the CAB ordered the railroad to divest itself of its holdings in EJA. While the railroad maneuvered in an attempt to find some legal device that would circumvent the ruling, Bevan poured in more money. In early 1968, EJA's European vice president, Carl Hirschmann, bought 90 percent of a small European airline named Transavia with the assistance of German financier Fidel Goetz. Again with Goetz's assistance, he also bought 70 percent of International Air Bahamas, a moribund line with landing rights in Nassau and Luxembourg. Although EJA leased to each line a 707, neither could be turned into a working proposition, and Hirschmann soon sold both of them to Ovid Anstalt, a Liechtenstein trust owned by the obliging Goetz. Goetz presently disposed of his new acquisitions, but his personal accounting showed him that somebody still owed him $4 million. He was not long in deciding who that somebody was.

In 1969, with domestic sources of capital having run dry, the railroad turned to a novel new form of financing, in the form of Eurodollars—a species of money that had hardly existed a decade before, and one that presented Goetz with a heaven-sent chance. A $10 million equipment rehabilitation loan was obtained from a Berlin bank that had evidently failed to do its homework, but not all of this windfall reached New York. Instead, the $10 million was diverted to the First Financial Trust of Liechtenstein, another Goetz entity; $4 million of it was then transferred to Videla Anstalt, yet another Goetz company, where it remained.

The railroad's lawyers for the transaction were Joseph and Francis Rosenbaum. According to a staff report of the House Committee on Banking and Currency, Francis Rosenbaum was later sentenced to ten years in jail for defrauding the U.S. Navy with, it seems, the assistance of Fidel Goetz. Earlier, in 1968, the Rosenbaums had received $1,125,000 from the railroad to develop sources of new funding. By an amazing coincidence, the money found its way straight to Goetz's account in a Liechtenstein bank, but it was returned on August 6. On August 28, the Rosenbaums transferred another $675,000 to a Liechtenstein account held in the name of the Agencier Industrial Corporation. The record does not say who controlled Agencier Industrial, and the money was not returned until July 21 of the following year. Not only had Goetz discovered a way of regaining the $4 million he claimed he was owed, but it seems that, with the connivance of the Rosenbaums, he and whoever controlled Agencier Industrial had discovered a way of laying their hands on substantial sums of the railroad's money. True, they eventually returned it, but clever men have always known how to make profitable use of other people's money. And in these days of electronic transfers and the vast expansion of the Euromarket, the possibilities are even more various than before.

In view of developments later in the decade, when the bankers finally figured out how to use the Eurocurrency market to circumvent the monetary policies of their governments, the peculations of the Rosenbaums and the looting of the equipment loan seem almost quaint. Certainly they are a very old-fashioned way of going about obtaining a large sum of money. With international bankers seized by a kind of madness following the huge OPEC deposits subsequent to 1973, shrewdly managed international construction companies like Fluor, Bechtel, and Ralph M. Parsons would discover that billions, not millions, could be made perfectly legally by selling vast quantities of overtechnologized junk to the eager Saudi Arabians. And, of course, smaller-scale operators of the stripe of Goetz and the Rosenbaums would find all sorts of ways to tap into deals. In the case of the Penn Central equipment loan, one sees an older kind of greed at work, one requiring naked theft. In these latter days of the OPEC-funded Euromarket, as we shall examine in a later chapter, no such crude methods are necessary: sums like $4 million are bus fare to the Saudis, and they dispense such sums all the time. The ironic result has been to keep many men honest who would otherwise steal.

And here is a further irony: given the predilection of the international bankers to give the Penn Central large amounts of cash without analyzing the company's books, if the railroad could only have held on until 1974 or 1975, it might have been able to pick up all the money it needed in the Euromarket, as easily as finding a nickel in the street. It happens all the time these days. The Penn Central's misfortune was one of bad timing. It had chosen the wrong time to go broke.

On October 14, 1969, three years after the investigation had begun, the CAB fined the Penn Central and EJA a total of $70,000. It was the second largest fine in CAB history. The agency also ordered total divestiture. The stock was eventually sold for $1,250,000; it had cost the railroad $328,000 in purchase money and $21 million in largely unrecoverable loans.

All told, the railroad's bold diversification program cost it in excess of $209 million, by the most conservative estimate. In return, it received both some opportunities to cook its books and a great big headache.

Nor have we finished. In partnership with the Madison Square Corporation, the Transportation Company owned the Madison Square Garden Center in New York. Through its subsidiary, the Pennsylvania Terminal Real Estate Corporation, it also owned 55 percent of a twenty-nine-story office building, Penn Plaza; Madison Square Garden and Tishman Plaza owned the balance. On December 18, 1968, in a complicated series of transactions, the railroad reduced its Penn Plaza holding, gave up a 25 percent equity interest in the Center, and forgave certain indebtedness. In return, the road received what eventually amounted to a 25 percent interest in the Madison Square Garden Corporation. On the face of it, the Penn Central gave up assets worth $.7 million in exchange for stock with an equity value of $4.2 million, but it was a paper transaction. Through the magic of bookkeeping (valuing the railroad's share of the Center at $1, for example, and fixing the worth of the real estate corporation's share of Penn Plaza at a cool $100), the Penn Central was able to report a net gain of $20,999,905, swelling the 1968 earnings report with a like amount of Chinese money. In fact, stock purchases over and above the exchange cost the railroad $2 million in some very real cash. An additional $2,802,000 was advanced to complete Penn Plaza, but by this time another $4.8 million was just the plink of another drop falling into the well of the railroad's doom.

In 1969, the New York Central Transportation Company, a wholly owned trucking subsidiary, seemed to pay the railroad a whopping $14.5 million in dividends: $6 million in April, another $6 million in June, and a final $2.5 million in December. Since N.Y.C. Transport only earned $4.2 million over the year, this was very nice money. After the railroad's collapse, the story was circulated that it had looted its subsidiary and left it prostrate, but this isn't quite what happened. Instead, using the books of the Manufacturers Hanover Trust Company, the railroad transferred $12 million (which it didn't have) to the trucking company and immediately transferred it back to itself, leaving the trucking company much as before, though saddled with the interest on a brand-new debt. (The additional $2.5 million appears to have been a genuine dividend.) The road pulled a similar trick with two other subsidiaries, Merchants Trucking and Penntruck, which were supposed to have kicked in with $300,000 and $1.7 million, respectively. It will come as no surprise to the diligent reader that the railroad paid the resulting $2 million to itself. It looked good on the books, though.

The railroad division owned 50 percent of Union Station in Washington, D.C.; the B & O owned the other half. The vehicle through which ownership was exercised was the Washington Terminal Company, which existed for no other purpose. In 1968, the federal government proposed to acquire the property for use as a National Visitor Center. On September 13, 1968, the board of directors of the Washington Terminal Company declared a dividend-in-kind, whereby undivided half interests in the property would be conveyed to two new companies, one of them owned by the PCR and the other owned by the B & O. The government would then lease the station for twenty-five years, but not until significant changes, estimated to take between two and three years, had been effected at the railroad's expense. The Penn Central then proceeded to declare that the dividend-in-kind was worth $11.7 million and so recorded it on its books, although no money had again changed hands and none was likely to for a considerable while. The sum amounted to around 13 percent of the railroad's consolidated net earnings for 1968. By way of an interesting footnote, the government actually did use the station as a visitor center for a while. It then served briefly as a shelter for the city's homeless. It presently stands empty, thundering with silence, a few exhibits drawn from American history adorning its walls. The most creative suggestion put forward for its use is to turn it back into a railroad station.

Meanwhile, David Bevan, the author of so much of this creative mischief, had a little game going on the side. This was Penphil, a club of gentlemen investors founded in 1962 by Bevan and the railroad's chief financial advisor, General Hodge. In time, the club's never very extensive membership came to include Bevan's brother, Thomas, five officers of his finance department, four officers and directors of the rail-road's subsidiaries, and Brig. Gen. Olbert Lassiter. The idea was to kick in a trifling sum—Bevan's contribution was $16,500—obtain some cheap bank money, and make a comfortable little killing. The bank money—at prime, without any pesky compensating balances (the money a borrower is usually required to deposit with the lending institution, usually in a sum equaling 20 percent of the indebtedness)—came largely from Chemical Bank of New York, and eventually totaled $1.8 million. The House Committee on Banking and Currency did not find the bank's logic too terribly hard to follow. The loans, its report stated, "were made on preferential terms, as compared to loans of a similar nature, because of the value to Chemical Bank of Penn Central's loan and deposit business. In effect, it was Penn Central's compensating balances, interest payments, and deposits that were subsidizing the Penphil line of credit for the personal profit of Penphil members."

Penphil's investment strategy was childishly simple in conception, although complex in execution. David Bevan controlled the investment policies of the Pennsylvania and later of the Penn Central. General Hodge was a man of diverse interests and contacts. Using inside information obtained either by Hodge or through the railroad, Penphil would invest in certain companies—Kaneb Pipeline, Great Southwest—often taking advantage of the leverage provided by the investments of the railroad (controlled by Bevan) or its subsidiaries in the same companies. Penphil would then sell its share at the proper psychological moment. Although Bevan later denied any wrongdoing or conflict of interest, it proved a very tidy business. In June 1970, Penphil made a cash profit of $226,895.51 and an unrealized paper profit of $3,026,476.40. David Bevan's original $16,500 had appreciated by 600 percent.

EJA and Penphil apart, all of this financial legerdemain

had but one obvious and suicidal purpose: to conceal the true state of the railroad. To some extent, it was an exercise in self-delusion. Bevan, with his keen knowledge of the truth contained within the books, seems not to have been too fooled, and Perlman was surely soon aware of the magnitude of the disaster, if not of his own curious part in it. As for the others—Saunders not least—they seemed to go forth into each new day like General Robert E. Lee, in the confident expectation of a miracle. Somehow the losses might be stemmed, somehow the railroad might make a profit, somehow replacing Perlman with a former telephone executive might turn the trick. Their jobs and reputations were at stake, and it is often true that the more a person has to lose, the greater his capacity for self-delusion. Unfortunately, the Penn Central Railroad was not the Army of Northern Virginia.

Amour-propre of the participants aside, there is another explanation, and it is not mutually exclusive. Paying dividends was madness, income maximization was a weapon that could turn in the hand, but they did do one thing: they bought time. That was a kind of madness, too, but there were reasons for it. Bevan might be able to swing one more bank loan, and the commercial paper had to hold up. In short, the incredible gyrations we have just witnessed, so reminiscent of the old vaudeville dance number known as "fire in a whorehouse," were designed to maintain the railroad's credit.

As anyone who has ever tried to balance a checkbook must surely be aware, maintaining the railroad's credit in this fashion made no objective sense whatever, but the PCR's terminal fascination with other people's money says much about the way business has come to be conducted in the latter half of the twentieth century, and it speaks volumes about the decade of rolling crises that the railroad's collapse ushered onto the stage of history. The facts of the case are simple enough. The railroad was falling apart, it didn't have any money, and a day of reckoning was not far off. It would seem, then, that the company's only rational option was to seek protection under Section 77 of the Bankruptcy Act—a section designed specifically for railroads, which allowed them to continue to function while, presumably, setting their house in order. It had happened often enough in the past; indeed, in the trough of the Depression, Section 77 bankruptcy had bid fair to becoming the preferred method of running a railroad. Moreover, the line had another string in its bow. It was essential to the commerce of its region, and the commerce of its region was essential to the economic well-being of the entire country. A collapse of its stock could trigger the nightmare of Western capitalism, a panic in the market. For these very good reasons, it seemed more than likely that the federal government would feel obliged to intervene in any serious discussion about the railroad's future—and the sooner the better.

Whether this intervention would take the form of a cash infusion, outright nationalization, or some other formula could not, of course, be predicted with any confidence. The railroad's chief officers would surely lose their jobs, but that was bound to happen anyway, one way or the other. When the end finally came, the government's solution was a dreary and halfhearted one, neither an outright nationalization nor a creative restructuring of the bankrupt northeastern roads, and the reluctant improvisations are with us to this day in the form of Conrail. Given a degree of candor on the part of the railroad and a measured response on the part of the government, matters could have been arranged in a considerably more orderly fashion, although by no means a perfect one; democracy simply doesn't work like that. The question is why the railroad made no move until it was almost too late.

The answer is a mixture of the old, the new, and the unique. First, the merger was supposed to work; it was supposed to save that $80 million. When it turned out that the merger was demonstrably *not* working, this was not construed as a sign that it could never work, and the books were adjusted to keep the flow of credit coming. When the merger

continued on its disastrous course, it was thought that cost-
cutting would do the trick and that a change in personnel
would help. Perlman went out, and Gorman came in, but the
time was long past for simple solutions. The railroad's officers
were now in a terrible bind: the merger still didn't work, the
merger was killing the company, but there was now all that
funny stuff on the balance sheets. To save themselves, or at
least to postpone a very personal day of reckoning, they had
to keep turning up fresh sources of other people's money.

There is nothing unusual about this line of thinking; potential bankrupts have sought to save themselves with the creative use of credit since the day money was invented. The fact
that the Penn Central was able to get away with it for as long
as it did, however, says much about the strange liberality of
the American banking community in the immediate post-
World War II period—a subject to which we shall return at
length in later chapters. Just as the nation shifted from coal to
oil in those years, so did the business world shift from hard
capital in the form of bond and stock offerings to soft capital
in the form of debt. There was a lot of money lying around in
the forties and fifties (and in the sixties, as we shall see, it
became possible to coin some when other sources dried up), it
gave the banks a business hitherto undreamed-of, and everybody succumbed to a kind of hypnosis that, if not entirely
sane, was exceedingly pleasant while it lasted. The banks
made back their interest, the business community obtained a
lot of cheap money, and the burden of debt piled up. It was
obvious that the Pennsylvania was in bad trouble just before
the merger. It was obvious that the combined roads had gone
completely haywire after the merger. At the same time, Saunders was issuing optimistic statements and producing balance
sheets that indicated everything was fine. To the bankers and
the sellers of commercial paper, this incongruity suggested
nothing for the longest time.

At the very last, there was a final compelling reason to
keep the road alive for a while longer. The banks needed time

to empty their trust departments of Penn Central stock. And certain of the railroad's officers needed time to dump their personal holdings.

On July 22, 1968, the ICC authorized the Penn Central to sell $100 million in commercial paper, a figure that was later raised to $200 million. The exclusive broker was the New York firm of Goldman, Sachs. Commercial paper consists of short-term promissory notes, sold either directly by the issuing company or through an intermediary. The purchaser is usually an institution, such as an insurance company or a college, other companies, endowments, and pension funds; very few individuals are involved in the market. At the time of the Penn Central issues, commercial paper was widely believed to be one of the safest investments in the land. It is hard to imagine why this was so; because the vast majority of the notes matured in less than 270 days, the issuers were spared the bothersome necessity of registering the issue with the Securities and Exchange Commission (SEC) and therefore did not have to make all sorts of disclosures about the state of their finances. Moreover, although commercial paper was supposed to be short-term financing, many companies (such as the Penn Central) found it possible to convert it into long-term debt by the simple expediency of rolling it as it came due—paying off the outstanding indebtedness with a new issue, something that could go on for as long as sufficient purchasers could be found. It is clearly a fragile system, easily shaken by a crisis of confidence, but the market grew vastly from 1960, when there was $4.5 billion in outstanding paper, to mid-1970, when the figure was $39.9 billion. In part, the confidence of the purchasers was based on the presumed integrity of the broker, the lines of bank credit presumably backing the issue, and (at the time) the rating given by the National Credit Office, a subsidiary of Dun & Bradstreet. In the case of the Penn Central, this confidence was sadly misplaced.

The chief analyst at the National Credit Office was dying;

the man he advised was inexperienced. The company continued to rate Penn Central paper as prime until June 1, 1970. Its principal excuse for doing so was the confidence Goldman, Sachs exhibited in the issue. Goldman, Sachs was aware of adverse developments at the railroad, but took the word of the management that things were working out. The brokerage therefore neglected to inform its customers that anything was a little bit amiss; as late as March 30, 1970, with the railroad tottering to the wall and its lines of credit depleted, Goldman, Sachs sold a small Pennsylvania college $300,000 of Penn Central paper. Presumably the college, like most other purchasers, eventually received 20 cents on the dollar. Earlier, in February, Goldman, Sachs had been able to persuade the railroad to repurchase $10 million of the paper in its inventory, cutting its own losses substantially.

The Penn Central began life with revolving bank credit of $100 million, a sum that was swiftly drawn down. Bevan went into the Euromarket and raised $50 million. He raised an additional $300 million in revolving credit by pledging Pennco's stock (its value artificially inflated by the shenanigans at Great Southwest) as collateral. He put together and sold a $50 million debenture offering backed by Pennco's holdings of Norfolk and Western stock. The money just disappeared. A second debenture offering of $100 million, put forth in early 1970, failed utterly. The railroad was losing more than $1 million a day; in the first quarter of 1970, it lost $101.6 million. A committee of directors delicately suggested that Saunders and Bevan step aside—so delicately, however, that Bevan and Saunders gave no indication of having understood what was being asked. The Great Southwest bubble burst and the price of its stock collapsed. The railroad was carrying $1.585 billion in long-term debt. Interest charges were running at $132 million a year. An additional $106 million in loans was due for repayment, and First National City Bank was owed $300 million for the drawn-down revolving credit. And $193.4 million in commercial paper was coming due. On January 27, Bevan approached First National City for a bridge loan to tide the company over until the $100 million debenture could be floated. The bank asked for more security. There wasn't any. Bevan then went to his friends at Chemical. Amazingly, they gave him the money, but after that the well was dry.

It became impossible to roll the commercial paper anymore, and a runoff began. Word of this, together with the disastrous first-quarter results, killed the bond offering forever. Bevan had run out of tricks. There was only one thing left to do. On April 30, Saunders met with John Volpe, Richard Nixon's secretary of transportation.

Even then, the railroad couldn't bring itself to come clean. At first it was suggested to Volpe and his aides that $50 million would turn the trick; after a bit of hemming and hawing, the figure was adjusted upward to $200 million, but anyone who knew the true condition of the railroad also knew that this was nowhere near enough, and that it was coming too late—if, indeed, it would come at all. As Volpe evolved his plan, the device that would make the loan possible was the Defense Production Act, which allowed such emergency aid under certain circumstances; the vehicle for the delivery of money would be the Department of Defense, which would guarantee the loan, while the money itself would come from the railroad's banks. A $750 million appropriation would then be passed by Congress to aid the nation's troubled railroads, Defense would be excused from its guarantee, and Transportation would shoulder the burden of saving the railroad with the appropriated money.

It was a wonderful plan, beautiful in its symmetry, but there were a few things wrong with it. It would take too long to implement. The $750 million had to be approved by the Democratic-controlled Congress, and Richard Nixon had just invaded Cambodia. Congress was therefore understandably reluctant to give Nixon anything, much less $750 million to save a giant railroad that had been reporting comfortable profits as recently as the end of the previous year. Volpe, who was beginning to comprehend the magnitude of the threatening disaster, might have prevailed upon the president to use the considerable leverage of his office to get things moving, but the president wasn't talking to him. Moreover, Nixon didn't understand the workings of American capitalism very well, despite the fact that he was supposed to be the guardian of it; his mind was on the massacre at Kent State and the upcoming congressional elections. The appropriation, if it was to reach the floor, had first to pass through the House Banking Committee, controlled by the old Texas populist Wright Patman, who hated banks, and the interim loan guarantee would be closely scrutinized by Mendel Rivers, who loved the Defense Department. Patman was sure to see the sinister hand of his ancient adversaries in the Penn Central request, and that was exactly what he did; he then called hearings. Rivers was equally certain to take steps to ascertain if the Defense Department would be left holding the bag, and the more he looked into the matter, the less he liked it. Moreover, there was no certainty whatever that the banks would advance the money even if Defense guaranteed it; the banks were very angry by now. And, as Patman suspected, they were up to something.

It required no great exercise of genius to see that the government initiative was too little coming too late in an environment where it couldn't possibly succeed in the first place, but it did have the effect of keeping the price of Penn Central stock from collapsing as word of the new disclosures about the company spread through the investing public. This does not mean there was a deliberate design; however, it is possible to make some observations. Stuart Saunders sat on the board of the Chase Manhattan Bank. David Bevan sat on the board of Provident National, as did John M. Seabrook, a director. John T. Dorrance, Jr. and Thomas L. Perkins, both directors, sat on the board of the Morgan Guaranty Trust. Eleven other directors likewise interlocked with other banks. By co-incidence, the Chase Manhattan, Morgan Guaranty, and Provident National were among the six banks that maintained major holdings of Penn Central stock in their trust departments. The others were Continental Illinois Bank and Trust, Security Pacific, and United States Trust, which had no direct interlocks with the PCR board, but a casual glance at the organization of the American banking community reveals a simply enormous number of indirect connections. It is, in fact, a splendid design for what old J. P. Morgan himself would have called a community of interest—something bank officers and directors are at pains to deny—and it was the possibility of entering just such a community (and obtaining an industrial espionage system) that was the chief reason urged upon John D. Rockefeller, Sr. in 1911, when his aides were persuading him to buy a bank.

Between May 1 and May 29, 1970, the six banks (and bank-connected Investors Mutual and the Allegheny Corporation) unloaded 776,792 shares of the Penn Central holdings, while the price per share slowly edged downward from 18⅝ to 12⅝—a serious decline, but nothing like what would have occurred if the truth had been known. Between June 1 and June 19, the last trading day before the bankruptcy, they divested themselves of an additional 436,000 shares as the stock—buoyed by word of a possible government rescue—hovered between 14 and 11⅛. The banks sold when the market rose and they sold when the market fell, meanwhile maintaining an outward appearance of optimism about the railroad's chances, which further stabilized the market.

It has been alleged but never proved that it was Stuart Saunders himself who warned the Chase. In any event, the collapse of the Penn Central was just about the only financial catastrophe of the 1970s in which the Chase failed to play its accustomed role of principal patsy. The banks later claimed that their trust officers were simply acting on information available to everyone—although they were trading against the optimistic trends in June (trends they did something to create)—and it is true that a number of brokers had twigged that all was not well at the PCR. Among these was the Philadelphia firm of Butcher & Sherred, headed by a former director and major stockholder named Howard Butcher III, who had long-established close ties to the road. Between March 30 and May 29, the brokerage disposed of more than 400,000 of its owner's and clients' shares. Goldman, Sachs, which continued to push the railroad's paper until the eleventh hour while persuading the railroad to buy back $10 million in unsold certificates, similarly unloaded more than 211,000 shares, and a few other brokers were likewise on the *qui vive*. It is equally true that nobody made any money from these transactions—as recently as July 1968, PCR stock had sold at a high of 86½—but, on the other hand, they saved something, which is more than can be said for many, many of the people who bought the shares they sold.

David Bevan had already looked after himself. In the first half of 1969, when the implications of what they had done began to sink in, he virtually halved his holding of the railroad's stock, selling 15,000 shares and (in the words of the SEC report) "managing to keep his personal fortune virtually intact." Other officers in the finance and real estate departments—the departments known as "Bevan's railroad"—followed suit, some of them commencing their sales as early as 1968. Bevan unloaded an additional 4,900 shares on June 19, 1970. Saunders, by contrast, held onto his personal 45,000 shares until the very last.

The end, when it came, was as remarkable for what didn't happen as for what did. Bevan, Saunders, and an embittered Perlman were out, relieved of their duties by the board of directors. Gorman, the Western Electric man, was in, but only long enough to preside over the wake. It was clear that no help was coming from Washington. The railroad had $7,308,130 in cash on hand. It was $748,974,342 in debt, and it could no longer pay its utility bills. There was no sense in continuing, and yet they couldn't seem to bring themselves to call it off. A special board meeting was called for Sunday, June 21. In an action strangely befitting the railroad's brief, surreal life, the directors devoted the first portion of their agenda to approving executive salaries and promoting Bevan's former assistant. Then they sat around and talked about the situation in Washington. Calls came in from Volpe and First National City's Walter Wriston. Wriston made it clear—as though he needed to—that no more bank money was going to be forthcoming without some form of guarantee. Volpe promised to try a last appeal to Nixon. While waiting for Volpe's next call, the board explored the possibility of retaining Saunders as a consultant of some sort. It was all very peculiar, almost as though nothing out of the ordinary was happening. Someone called a judge and asked him to stand by. Volpe called again at 5 P.M. Nixon still wouldn't speak to him. With the largest railroad in the country on the brink of an abyss from which only he could save it, the president of the United States wasn't answering his telephone. It was all over. At 5:40, Judge C. William Kraft, Jr., acting from his home, signed the order placing the Penn Central Railroad under Section 77 of the Bankruptcy Act.

A great many things then occurred, and the upshot of them all was that nothing happened. The railroad did not grind to a halt; it simply dwindled away. Amtrak took over its intercity passenger service in 1971 and immediately began paring away at the long-haul routes that Perlman and Saunders—and Symes, before them—had petitioned to abandon for so long and so fruitlessly. A full decade and some billions of dollars of the taxpayers' money later, Amtrak has yet to make a profit, which is no big surprise; no national passenger network does. In 1976, Conrail took over the railroad's Philadelphia headquarters and its freight and commutation business, along with considerable portions of the Ann Arbor, the Reading, the Lehigh Valley, the Central of New Jersey, the

Lehigh and Hudson, and that venerable cripple, the Erie Lackawanna. After a good deal of cutting and trimming, Conrail ended up with 17,000 miles of track (3,000 less than Penn Central ran on merger day), a lot of uneconomic labor contracts, many thousands of disgruntled commuters, and a whopping annual deficit that is only now responding to the benefits of surgery and a rich poultice of public money. The Penn Central survives as an investment company. It recently showed signs that it may one day thrive.

There was no panic. The railroad's collapse triggered a $3 billion sell-off in commercial paper, which could have been very, very bad, but for once the Federal Reserve was ready. Although the machinery had never been used in quite that way before—certainly not in 1929, or the economic history of the country might have been very different—the Fed let it be known that, come Monday, June 22, the discount window would be wide open. That is, any bank that needed money to tide over a company during the commercial paper runoff could get it from the Fed. On Tuesday, Regulation Q—which limits the rate that banks can pay for deposits—was amended, and more money flowed into the system. Chrysler was particularly hard hit, but with the Fed responding boldly, Manufacturers Hanover was able to raise the company's credit line, thus postponing its day of reckoning for another decade.

It was widely agreed that the Penn Central crisis was the Fed's finest hour; but the Fed's bold and timely action did much to obscure the fact that its clients, the banks, were busy learning nothing and forgetting everything from what ought to have been a salutory lesson—albeit one that might have triggered the long-feared domino effect in the world financial markets that would have duplicated the disaster of 1929–32. Under the circumstances, it is a little hard to fault the Fed for saving civilization as we know it. For once in its long and checkered career, the Fed was doing exactly what its founders had designed it to do; in the unruly decade that followed, it would never do so again.

Still, in the orgy of self-congratulation that followed, it was lost on almost everybody but Congressman Patman that the banks had deemed a flagrantly mismanaged corporation worthy of $750 million in credit, that in doing so they had failed to scrutinize its books with the same baleful eye they routinely cast upon the finances of humbler but infinitely more solvent applicants—shoe salesmen, for example—that in Penphil they had generously underwritten what looks perilously close to a conflict-of-interest scam (which should also have told them something about the company), and that when the company began to run down the lines of credit it needed to back its commercial paper, they did nothing. But Congressman Patman had been an enemy of the banks for a very long time and he had said many things and no one was predisposed to listen to him now.

The fall of the Penn Central was an old-fashioned bankruptcy in the classical sense: the company ran out of money, and it went broke. Because it was an enormous bankruptcy, its butcher's bill was long, and it has not yet been fully paid. It was the sort of thing that lawyers sometimes dream of after three martinis; at the time, it was predicted that the legal docket resulting from the bankruptcy itself and the subsequent creation of Conrail might finally be cleared by the end of the century. Things have moved a little faster than that, but not much. And, of course, the chaos caused by the merger, the crisis of confidence caused by the bankruptcy, and the cutbacks, uncertainty, and continuing service problems of Conrail have done nothing to arrest the decline of the industrial Northeast; in that sense, the damage done by the Penn Central, simply by existing, has been incalculable. It destroyed a viable road—the Central—while merely postponing the fate of the Pennsy. And it was fifty years too late. As Pierpont Morgan saw clearly, a community of interests among the railroads was not only desirable, it was logical, and as time went on, it became essential. The time to have created the Penn

Central or something like it came and went in the 1920s, as the Federal Railroad Administration wound down its work and the first signs of trouble began to appear. By 1969, with the Pennsy on its last legs and the Central desperate about its subsidized competition, the Penn Central was not only illogical but impossible, and not even Alfred Perlman could save it.

It was the first great bankruptcy of the decade; it was the last of the classical bankruptcies as they are commonly understood; and it contained the seeds of a bleak future. The railroad went broke because it ran out of ordinary money, but it also played the commercial paper market and lost, nearly bringing the economic system down with it, and it toyed with a strange new form of money, called Eurodollars. In the dust and confusion and self-congratulation following the railroad's fall, the larger implications of the commercial paper crisis were all but ignored, for there would have been no commercial paper crisis if the liquidity of the entire system had not been impaired; many, many companies were using paper in just the same way as the Penn Central, and on the day of reckoning, they got caught. Nor was much made of the fact that, when all domestic lines of credit had utterly dried up and the railroad's credit wasn't worth a plugged nickel, it was able to raise millions in the Euromarket with surprising ease. In the not-so-very-distant future, the Euromarket would grow to astonishing size. It would also continue to make a practice of loaning money blindly to cripples, and the world order would be in peril.

No one could have foreseen that, of course—no one but the oil companies thought much about oil then or where a lot of it came from—but a hint had been given, and it should have suggested something. Early in the nineteenth century, Alexis de Tocqueville described the United States as a country of businessmen ruled by a Congress of lawyers, but times change. The Congress is still full of lawyers and the economy is still full of businessmen, but in a time of mounting debt, the half-understood policies of a handful of banks have come to dominate the councils of lawyer and corporate bureaucrat alike. Unnoticed by all but a few mavericks like Texas Congressman Wright Patman (an old man from a different time, who had been wrong too often) and a handful of paranoiacs of the right and left (who were disqualified from the debate), the rules of business were changing in wondrous ways. Control of the nation's economy was slipping away from the caucus room and the corporate suite, concentrating instead in the hands of those very men who had money to lend—and who, when the vast windfall of the OPEC billions fell into their laps, were to export their policies and their mistakes to the world. Another half-dozen years would pass before the crisis broke. But before then, there would be ample warning, and it would be ignored.

2.

Grant's Tomb

Happy companies are all alike, but bankrupt companies each go bankrupt in their own way. When W. T. Grant filed for protection from its creditors under Chapter 11 on October 1, 1975, it entered the record books as the largest mercantile failure in American history, second only to the Penn Central on the scale of corporate calamity. At the time it occurred, however, it had almost come to seem that declaring bankruptcy was just another of the things that large monied structures did, like making tires or collecting garbage.

New York City's long romance with the more fanciful possibilities of double-entry bookkeeping was over; the city's till was empty at last, its string had run out, and if it was compelled to default on its obligations—as seemed likely—the consequences would be incalculable. The Franklin National Bank had gone under the previous year, in large part the victim of the schemes of the Italian manipulator Michele Sindona; it was the largest bank failure in American history. The Real Estate Investment Trust bubble (of which we shall hear more in connection with the Chase Manhattan Bank) was about to burst, and before the nation celebrated its two-hundreth birthday more banks would fail than at any time since the Great Depression, many fine old names would disappear forever, and the first OPEC oil price rise would create a slow but increasingly alarming emergency in the vicinity of the Brazilian national debt. It isn't going too far to say that, beginning with the collapse of the Penn Central and the dreary end of the go-go years on the stock markets, American capitalism entered into its second great crisis in this century.

It was an odd sort of crisis. For one thing, it was cumulative rather than sudden; each aspect seemed to be fenced off from every other aspect. There was no single great shock but rather a series of shocks, played out over a considerable time, which meant that the defenses put in place during the New Deal and earlier could more effectively be deployed and the insult to the system as a whole could be more readily managed with accepted techniques and successful improvisations. It was as though an alcoholic were suffering a series of nonfatal medical setbacks rather than getting himself run over by a truck.

Moreover, the true nature of the crisis was so complicated that it was incredibly difficult to figure out just what the hell was going on. President Gerald Ford gave no indication of understanding the nature of the situation, much less its gravity, and neither did his successor. A stock market crash may have complex causes, but its effects are remarkably simple, among them panic, depression, and unemployment. By contrast, an epidemic of bankruptcy and near-bankruptcy is extremely confusing, especially if much of the relevant information is locked up in institutions—such as banks, such as the office of the comptroller of the currency—where secrecy is perceived as a prized necessity, and the information that does happen to be available is as incomprehensible as Pushtu.

Some of the repercussions of Grant's collapse were predictable. Some of the blunders leading to its downfall were so incredible that a child can comprehend them and predict their effects. But the largest blunder of all—the blunder that made all the rest possible—proved to be something of a purloined letter, so obvious that it became invisible. It only required a little thought about something called the Fed Funds market. Unfortunately, almost nobody but the bankers even knew the Fed Funds market existed.

Superficially, the Grant bankruptcy seemed to follow the pattern made familiar by the Penn Central: a worsening profits picture, a commercial paper runoff, the dismissal of officers, desperate attempts to reorganize, and collapse. In fact, the circumstances were very different. Simply put, the Penn Central's woes were caused by Saunders' ill-conceived attempt to use the Central to save the Pennsy and turn the resulting company into a conglomerate, whereas the debacle at Grant was the direct result of some of the worst decisions ever made in a major executive suite, decisions that were abetted by some of the largest banks in the land.

Founded by William T. Grant in Lynn, Massachusetts, in 1906, the chain spent the first years of its existence happily coining money by selling slipcovers and picture frames to the wives of the industrious workingmen of blue-collar America. Woolworth's and S. S. Kresge were five-and-dime stores; Bill Grant's early motto was "Nothing over 25¢" and he was as good as his word. With enormous exuberance and a distinct flair for the dramatic, he sold odd lots and half sets and any sort of bargain he could pick up from the warehouses; he once picked up a shipment of damaged straight razors, had them rehoned, and sold them for a quarter each. When he expanded, he did so with care. Aware that he couldn't be everywhere at once, he allowed his local managers considerable latitude in their purchase of merchandise so that they could take advantage of any local coups that would bring confusion to the competition, but at the same time he was concerned about inventory control, the need to know what was in his stores, what was selling, and what was gathering dust on his shelves. The old saw to the contrary, nobody makes any money selling iceboxes to the Eskimos. Profit margins in retailing are low at the best of times, and the idea is to sell everything you have, sell it quick, buy some more stuff, and sell it again. This strategy is so basic that it verges on the simple-minded, although implementing it in practice isn't nearly as easy as it seems; it is mentioned here, with the reader's indulgence, only because of what happened next.

Thus was Bill Grant's fortune made. He identified a market and he sold things to it, and it made him a rich man. He stepped down from active management in 1952, but he hung around and kept an eye on things until 1966, when he finally and totally retired at the age of ninety. It is interesting that things did not begin to go badly haywire until the old tycoon's hand finally left the throttle, although there were some earlier signs that all was no longer as it should be. Grant's successor was his brother-in-law, William Staley. Like all new brooms, Staley wanted to show what he was made of. Like his relative, he had some ideas. Unlike his relative, he couldn't quite make up his mind just what those ideas were. He was now the head of a chain of variety stores. Montgomery Ward and J. C. Penney were making a tidy sum as department stores. Perhaps that was the way to go. On the other hand, K Mart was making it big as a discounter. And, of course, the original Grant concept wasn't to be sneezed at; it made money, too. After a good deal of toing-and-froing with Louis C. Lustenberger (Grant's president from 1959 to 1968), an uneasy combination of all three was arrived at: your local W. T. Grant would be a discount, department, and variety store, which created a certain confusion in the mind of the buying public—it was a little hard to tell just what Grant was, anyway. Still, no very great harm was done. The company continued to prosper, blurred though its image was, it being difficult (but not, of course, impossible) to avoid making money in the 1960s, especially if you were as established and well sited as Grant's. And it was precisely here, in the locations of the stores, that Staley decided to make his mark.

Between 1963 and 1973, Staley opened 612 new stores. In sixty years in the business, Bill Grant had expanded his chain to 601 stores and made a pretty penny; in a single decade, his

brother-in-law doubled the size of the chain (with a little help
from his friends at the banks) and lost the company's shirt. Of
Staley's 612 new stores, 317 were opened in 1969–70, three
years after the founder's departure; in October 1969, the
chain opened 15 in a single day. At the start of the expansion,
the chain was making about $40 million a year after taxes; in
1973, with 1,213 stores in operation, it grossed in the vicinity
of $1.8 billion, but its net remained virtually the same, at
$37.8 million. Then the roof fell in.

In a near-classic example of the wisdom of the penny and
the foolishness of the pound, many of the new Grant stores
were located in the most economical locations—economical in
the sense that they were cheaply bought or cheaply leased. In
practice, this meant that they were badly placed, in smaller
shopping centers somewhat off the beaten track or in centers
where the market was already saturated. Many of the new
stores were also of the larger Grant City variety, with between 50,000 and 70,000 square feet of floor space as distinct
from the older stores, with around 30,000 square feet. To fill
up the space (pursuing the confusing policy of a little of this, a
little of that), the chain went heavily into what are known in
the trade as big-ticket items, appliances and furniture. Unfortunately, it did so just as the size of the American family began to shrink drastically and real estate prices were taking off,
which in combination meant that there was less call for furniture, fewer people could afford a house, and the appliance
market began to take a beating. (Condominium developers,
needless to say, did not shop at Grant.)

In order to enable their customers to afford the big-ticket
items, the chain went heavily into consumer credit—to the
point that it became, in the words of one of its unhappy bankers, a finance company with a retail appendage. The majority
of Grant's customers didn't have checking accounts. It therefore became necessary to establish local offices where they
could pay their bills—and paying their bills turned out to be
something they didn't do as often as management had ex-

pected. Credit checks were almost nonexistent—"if a customer's breath would fog a mirror, he got credit," one executive described the company's card-issuing policy. Clerks were given a dollar for every creditor they could sign up, and at least one store manager who attempted to protest the insanity of it all was told to shut up or lose his job. New York headquarters seemed to have lost its mind.

It is conventional wisdom in the trade that a new store takes between three and four years to earn back a profit—if, indeed, it ever earns one. Opening 612 stores in a decade, more than half of them in a single year, and 15 of them in a single day, is therefore a species of lunacy unless you happen to have bottomless pockets, and Grant didn't. Instead, in a wondrous demonstration of Santayana's adage about the lessons of history, it was funding its expansion by issuing and rolling commercial paper backed with inadequate lines of bank credit. In the aftermath of the Penn Central-inspired runoff of commercial paper, it is hard to say which is more remarkable: that Grant's financial wizards thought they could get away with it, or that insurance companies and other institutions continued to purchase the stuff—but their brief, tempestuous romance with Grant was not the end of their unwisdom.

Despite the Penn Central disaster, despite what subsequently happened at Grant, companies continued to issue paper and treat it as long-term debt by rolling it forward right up to the very end of the seventies, and institutions and companies went right on buying it. The end result was a rather nasty surprise for the Federal Reserve (and all the rest of us) at the end of the decade, when the Fed attempted to do something about inflation by making money very expensive. Here was the nasty surprise: because so much money had escaped into commercial paper from the banking system, when former investors in that paper became enchanted with the new high-yielding Treasury bills and money market funds, the companies that had grown accustomed to treating paper as long-term debt had to find another source of funds, and only one existed. It was the banking system. And as a major portion of the nation's corporate debt sought to come back to Mother, money became not merely expensive, it became very, very expensive. In the early eighties it began to look as though money would never become cheap again. This was hardly what the Fed had intended, but it was what the Fed got.

The administration of the original harsh medicine was a little complicated and many things were involved in it, but basically it was supposed to work in the following way: Expensive money means high interest rates. High interest rates, in turn, are supposed to retard the growth of credit. The expansion of credit is, to a degree, the private minting of new money. Conventional banker's wisdom states that a deposit can be lent six times; that is, it can be used to generate loans six times its size. Much of this money is fictitious in that it consists of the transfer of some numbers from one set of books to another set of books; as long as money limits its activity to the closed confines of the banking system, nothing happens. Eventually, however, some of it is going to get itself spent (otherwise there is no point in borrowing it in the first place), and at that point we encounter something called the multiplier effect, since the very act of spending lent money increases the amount of money in circulation.

Moreover, American banks usually require something called a compensating balance. That is, the borrower is usually required to keep a certain proportion of the loan—often around 20 percent—on deposit as a way of compensating the bank for the favor of the loan and an earnest of his intention to repay it. Since it is a deposit, the bank will therefore lend it; as dedicated followers of Cotton Mather, bankers hold that anything that is not useful is vile, and there is nothing less useful to a banker than an unlent deposit, which also costs the bank money in the form of interest.

Observe what has happened. A deposit is lent upwards

six times. Some of this money (usually most of it, eventually, but in dribs and drabs) escapes from the banking system and finds its way into what one might call the secular economy, where it increases the amount of money in circulation. At the same time, the bank has required the borrower to maintain a compensating balance, which means, in effect, that the bank has lent itself a deposit. This money, too, is lent upwards of six times, further increasing the amount of money in circulation. An increase in the money supply is a good way of causing inflation.

The borrower's role in all of this is to pay as little for the money as possible. The banker's role is to keep his books in some sort of rough balance; it is not the least of the things that he does to earn his salary. As for the Fed, its job is to keep the whole thing from getting out of hand, as it will surely do if the greasing of the skids of commerce is left solely in the hands of everybody else's profit motive. One way the Fed can accomplish its task is by upping the reserve requirement; that is, the amount of deposits the Fed can order a national bank to hold immobile and unlent. Bankers understandably hate the reserve requirement, and, as we shall see in a subsequent chapter, they have been doing something about it. Another string in the Fed's bow is its control over the price of money. Confronted with double-digit inflation at the end of the 1970s, the Fed decided to make money very expensive indeed.

Bankers hate expensive money too; expensive money is bad for business. At the end of the 1970s, however, certain things combined to bring about a unique situation. Since money was now expensive, the money market itself—the buying of Treasury bills and other interest-bearing paper—became an attractive proposition to corporations and individuals with spare cash to invest, especially because it had all the delusive earmarks of being the sort of sure thing commercial paper was once perceived to be. At the same time, the slump in the automobile industry and in the industrial Northeast in general—the latter caused, in part, by the chaos resulting

from the Penn Central merger—afflicted corporate and institutional treasurers with a measure of disenchantment. As a
result, they began to run down (that is, reduce or eliminate)
their holdings of commercial paper. As it happened, the sin
of treating commercial paper as long-term debt was not peculiar to the Penn Central and Grant; many, many companies
were hooked on the stuff. Now the market was going sour
again, and there was only one place to turn: to the banks,
whose money the Federal Reserve had just made extremely
expensive.

It ought to be axiomatic that no bank will charge 20 percent interest on a loan unless it can get the money, but it
doesn't seem to be; a great many people appear to believe
that astronomical interest rates, persisting over months and
years, are the result of some cruel whimsy, and Congressman
Wright Patman is no longer on the scene to ferret out the
truth. In fact, congestion at the loan window (in part caused
by the Fed's effect on the money market) combined with expensive cash (created by the inflation fighters at the Fed)
pushed interest rates to heights seldom dreamed of outside
the Mafia, drove up the price of the goods manufactured with
all that exorbitant borrowed capital, and partially destabilized
the economies of Western Europe. It may very well be true
that man is superior to the beasts because he can foresee the
consequences of his acts, but here, as is so often the case, an
exception seems to have been made for the world of high
finance.

In the case of W. T. Grant, it should have been obvious
that some very bad trouble was brewing; a child could have
seen it. By early 1974, its short-term debt had reached $493.2
million, and perilously much of that sum was in commercial
paper. It was not only expanding too rapidly and in ways that
flew in the face of rudimentary logic, but inventory control
had gone to hell. Managers were required to report only aggregate sales; New York headquarters no longer had the
faintest idea of what merchandise was selling and what

merchandise was gathering dust and taking up space—and New York headquarters didn't seem to care. Traditionally, 20 percent of Grant's items had accounted for 80 percent of its business, but nobody knew if that was still true or not and if so, which 20 percent was moving. The vast majority of Grant's customers were women, and one of the first retailing lessons Bill Grant had learned was that you can't sell to your customer unless you can get her into your store. This is best accomplished by placing enticing merchandise in the front of the establishment. The merchandise in the front of the new Grant and Grant City stores was men's clothing. (The man who was given the hopeless task of untangling the mess remarked later, "I'm surprised they didn't have tires up there.") Mr. Grant's policy of allowing his managers a reasonable degree of purchasing autonomy had gone haywire, too; in a gesture of lèse majesté that boggles the mind, the new management allowed its managers to purchase upwards of four-fifths of all their merchandise and price it as they pleased, which meant that Grant stores in the same area sometimes ended up competing with each other. It was only a matter of time before the whole gaudy edifice would come tumbling down, and that moment came with typical swiftness.

Grant ended its fiscal year on January 31, which meant that fiscal 1974 began on February 1, 1973. In 1973, the nation's economy began to nose down into the long, queasy dive that would culminate with the horror stories of the bicentennial year. Grant had reported earnings of $37.8 million for fiscal 1973, although this figure, like the Penn Central's, was later called in question. In fiscal 1974, earnings dropped to $8.4 million, and eight banks were called upon for a $100 million loan which, astonishingly, they granted. The earnings decline was followed by a $7 million loss in the first quarter of the new fiscal year. The board of directors rose in revolt. Staley and his successor as chairman, Richard W. Mayor, resigned from the company. James G. Kendrick, who had been exiled to the Canadian subsidiary when he protested the disas-

trous initiatives of the sixties, was brought in as chairman.
Moody's and Standard & Poor yanked the company's credit
rating and a runoff of its commercial paper began. By August,
Grant was effectively out of money. Its suppliers were getting
nervous, and ominous references to the Penn Central began
to appear in the financial press. Losses for the first six months
reached $10.9 million. The dividend was omitted.

The financial community now came to the rescue. Led by
Morgan Guaranty Trust, Chase Manhattan, and Citicorp—
each of which chipped in with $97 million—an unwieldy con-
sortium of 143 banks advanced the company $600 million. A
rescue operation involving 143 banks is not merely unwieldy,
it is unworkable. There are too many different corporate priorities involved, too little coordination, and eventually—inevitably—the junior partners decided to take their money and
run. But 143 banks represented Grant's principal creditors,
and it was said that the Fed had insisted. The Fed denied this
but admitted that it was watching the situation. There was
reason to worry. In 1974, the country was already sufficiently
traumatized by the long twilight of Richard Nixon. Although
there was much self-congratulation on the subject of how well
James Madison's Constitution had worked, there were
grounds to question whether the country even had a government anymore, much less an economic policy. There were
doubts about the, er, intellectual capacity of Gerald Rudolf
Ford; the country had not yet experienced Jimmy Carter. The
danger posed by a collapse of Grant seemed very real. Grant
had retrenched a little, but with 1,172 stores and 78,000 employees, it was still huge. It had 8,000 suppliers, some of them
marginal and dependent on the company for survival. Grant's
shopping centers were badly situated, but Grant dominated
them; without the magnetic power of the big Grant stores, the
satellite shops might go under too, creating a domino effect.
True, the worst had failed to come to pass when the Penn
Central went under, but it was dangerous to regard it as a

precedent, especially with the country's executive branch in a state of flux.

And yet. Grant was in terrible shape, and a major part of its collateral was dubious. The $600 million loan was secured by Grant's 51 percent interest in Zeller's, its profitable Canadian subsidiary, and by its accounts receivable. Unfortunately, many of those accounts receivable were fairy gold in the form of uncollectable charge-card balances, and the rest of them depended on the continued goodwill of Grant's suppliers and their factors—companies that do the suppliers' bookkeeping and collect their bills. The suppliers and the factors were not in a happy mood. "I doubt very much we'd be where we are now if we had been aware of the true situation from the start," remarked a Morgan vice president somewhat later, with the gift of hindsight. Still, it is a remarkable statement. The nature of the company's problems was well known, and another Morgan vice president sat on its board. One might almost think that it had a guilty conscience, if a bank were capable of such a thing, but no bank is.

The presence of the Morgan at the death of Grant—not only as a leading bank but increasingly as spokesman for the creditors—offers an interesting example of symmetry. In its final apotheosis, Grant was the very image of commercial suburbia, with its huge barnlike stores on their acres of asphalt—the death blow to so many central cities and so much that was good or, at least, better. Usually it is the federal government, with its highways and mortgage policies, that takes the rap for the more hideous aspects of the suburban experience, but this is to reckon without something called the Fed Funds market.

In their most basic form, Fed Funds are simply surplus bank money, and the market consists of matching that surplus with some other bank's deficit—i.e., a bank with a little spare money transfers it (for a consideration) to another bank with insufficient funds to satisfy its loan customers. The Fed Funds market flourished in the twenties, died out in the thirties, and was reinvented in the fifties to fill a highly specific need of, at that moment in history, the Morgan Bank.

The Morgan is a wholesale bank, as all great banks were once wholesale banks. That is, it confines itself to what might be called big-ticket customers, large entities like corporations that require large sums of money for relatively short periods of time. As a way of doing business, this has some very considerable advantages. By dispensing with a host of small depositors and the small-loan trade, the Morgan avoids the many ills that retail banking is heir to—the bothersome and redundant paperwork, the tedious shuffling of small sums around, the expense of maintaining a lot of branches, and, not least, the necessity of giving mortgages.

Domestic mortgages are one of the most stable forms of debt known to man; a family will give up many things before it gives up its home. Unfortunately for the lending institution that issues them, however, mortgages tie up money for what, to a bank, is an enormous period of time and at a rate of return that is usually inflexible. In banking, as in most businesses, the big profits are made through speed and flexibility, moving money as fast as possible at the most favorable possible terms, and until very recently in this country, no great bank wanted to get involved with the average citizen and his complex needs. Mortgages, savings accounts, and other such business were the province of the small bank, the savings bank, and the savings and loan institution.

As a resolutely wholesale institution, therefore, the Morgan found itself badly placed when the Fed first shut off the flow of cheap and easy money in the 1950s as the Eisenhower administration attempted to tighten up the currency. Other great banks, following the lead of the Bank of America, could tap the surprisingly large reservoir of cash deposited in those boom years by their least significant customers. The Morgan couldn't, and it reinvented the Fed Funds market instead.

The trick was easily done. All the Morgan (and, presently, its many imitators) had to do was locate a bank, usually a smaller bank, with some extra money, purchase the money at a premium, and—in the beginning—run the transaction through the books of the Federal Reserve. Hence the name. At first, after a certain amount of waffling, the Fed decided to treat these transfers as loans and therefore as subject to the Fed's single-borrower restrictions, but in 1963, James Saxon, John Kennedy's controversial comptroller of the currency, decided that they were purchases and therefore free of those restrictions. The market grew apace, was further refined to eliminate the need for the Fed, and—as it happened—was reaching its first maturity just as W. T. Grant developed a pressing need for some lines of credit.

Most banks in the money centers of New York, Chicago, and San Francisco trade in Fed Funds. They're a handy way of evading the reserve requirement, since such purchases of money are not deemed to constitute a portion of the relevant bank's reserves. From the bankers' point of view they help to keep the money situation pleasingly fluid in times of tight money, thus enabling them to thwart the will of the Federal Reserve. But Fed Funds also do something else. Because a great many of the transactions involve the movement of money at premium rates from midrank and smaller regional banks to the money centers, Fed Funds have become a principal way of circumventing one of the great purposes the Federal Reserve was founded to fulfill.

The founders of the system were acutely aware that there was a danger posed by the fluidity of money. Money has no regional identity. Like nature, it abhors a vacuum. It flows to wherever it is needed, since those are the very places where it can command a handsome price for its services. In practice, this means that it flows to the money centers, with their enormous capital requirements, sophisticated institutions, and great immediate profits. The danger, then, was that the provinces would be stripped of their development money in the form of bank deposits; and for this reason, twelve Federal Reserve banks were established, three in the money centers

and the rest scattered around the country, regulating the flow
of capital.

The Fed Funds market is an obvious end run around this
commendable goal, since the cash flows to the money centers
anyway, which means that regional depositors end up subsidizing their competition and unwittingly conspiring in their
own destruction. To understand how the trick is done, let us
take the example of a retail merchant in a middling American
city. He keeps his reserves in his local bank. He also maintains his payroll accounts there, and numbers of his more prudent employees doubtless maintain savings accounts there as
well. These deposits constitute a portion of his region's liquid
wealth, and deposits exist to be loaned. The retailer is therefore perfectly justified in anticipating that when he needs to
borrow some money for expansion, maintenance, or to meet
some emergency—just such an emergency as might be posed
by the arrival of a big, cost-cutting W. T. Grant—the money
will be forthcoming from the local financial institution he and
merchants like him have done so much for over the years.
(His employees probably share similar expectations when it
comes to mortgages and home-improvement loans. Many of
them are in for an even bigger surprise, especially if they are
black and dwell in the inner city.) Thanks to the Fed Funds
market, however, there exists a pernicious likelihood that his
local financial institution's money has gone a-wandering to
build condominiums in Florida or to subsidize the Brazilian
foreign trade deficit or to swell the bulging coffers of the Euromarket . . . or to build a W. T. Grant department store.
This doesn't mean that he won't get his money—local banks
can buy funds, too—but it does mean that it will be more
expensive, the terms may be otherwise unfavorable, and there
may not be enough of it, placing him at an immediate competitive disadvantage.

Nor is he precluded from going to the money centers
himself, but there his problems will be similar if not worse.
He isn't large enough to command the prime rate and the

most favorable payback; he may be badly placed in an obsolete downtown location (obsolete, that is, in terms of the
reshaping of the American landscape being accomplished, in
part, by the creative use of his own deposits); he may not get
the money at all; and if he does get it, he may be forced to
relocate in self-defense.

To summarize, then: in their wholesale business, large
money-center banks prefer to make the largest possible loans
to the largest entities and to receive their money back as
swiftly as possible. Thanks to the Morgan's reinvention of the
Fed Funds market, many of these sums come from the deposits of regional banks, deposits whose source is regional
business and regional salaries. With a beautiful and madden-
ing kind of circularity, these deposits are then used to bank-
roll the local business' most powerful competition, either
regionally, in another area like the Sunbelt, or even abroad,
to the growing disadvantage of the place where the money
came from to begin with. It is a game that can even be played
within the narrow confines of the money centers themselves,
as for example in the progressive disinvestment by the banks
in the industrial base of Brooklyn or the South Side of Chicago. In the history of the Fed Funds market one sees written
much of the economic history of the last twenty years as well
as the strange reorganization of the national landscape. What
one witnesses here is a form of pillage.

And in 1974–75, as Grant was collapsing, the banks were
expanding this practice to a global scale. The first of the two
great oil shocks came in 1973. By 1974, the Euromarket was
glutted with funds stripped from the consumers and industrial-
ists of Japan and the West. Following the same pattern developed in Fed Funds, the banks were then—learning nothing
from the salutory lesson right before their eyes—to pursue the
same pattern, lending the largest possible loans to the largest
possible entities. Next they were going to try to get their
money back. Even as Grant was struggling for survival, the
Morgan and a few other giant institutions were redistributing

the spoils of OPEC to whole countries in the Third World,
forgetful of two things. One, many of the countries they were
lending to (and receiving money from) were corrupt, irrational, and unable to pay their debts; two, when a country
goes bankrupt, unlike a company, its assets cannot be seized
and sold.

In the case of Grant, the banks—led by the Morgan—
were about to take some of these funds and do more.
They were about to ride a dying horse until it dropped.

The company's third-quarter loss rose to $11.6 million,
197 percent greater than the previous year's $3.9 million
shortfall. Attempts were made to calm the fears of the suppliers and the factors, and it was announced that sixty-six unprofitable branches would be closed. But things kept getting
worse. In the overall fiscal year, the chain lost $177 million,
about 62 percent of it due to bad debt on credit cards. After
Penn Central's disastrous showing in 1971 and Anaconda's
$365 million write-off after its Chilean copper holdings were
nationalized by the Allende government, it was the third
largest business loss in American history.

The first $75 million repayment on the $600 million loan
was put off for six months, to June 2, 1975, but the smaller
banks in the consortium were growing concerned. In what increasingly began to look like a slow liquidation, the company
announced that it would close an additional 222 stores. The
idea was to trim the most obvious losses, pick up a little
money by selling the leases, and reduce the chain's huge off-
balance-sheet debt, which existed in the form of its contracts
with the landlords who actually owned the real estate and the
equipment—a sum in excess of $1 billion, payable until 1995
and beyond. Like most major chains, Grant didn't actually
own its stores. It leased them from real estate combines, and
the money owed under the contracts, while it was a genuine
debt, wasn't aggregated on the company's annual balance
sheet as such, any more than the renter of an apartment lists

his total leasehold rent as a debt. Nevertheless it was there, it was owed, and the landlords, like the suppliers, the factors, and the smaller banks, wanted their money.

The twenty-seven largest banks in the consortium agreed to extend their portion of the short-term loan to March 1976. The smaller banks wanted their $56 million back, and they wanted it by June 2. Robert H. Anderson, Sears' aggressive vice president of retail merchandising, was brought in as the new president on a five-year contract that would pay him $1.25 million by 1980 and $100,000 a year thereafter for the rest of his life, the salary guaranteed by the banks. In many ways, Anderson was another Alfred Perlman: an innovative whiz with a great reputation; if anyone could save the company, he could. He was a throwback to the romantic period of American business, before the evolution of corporate bureaucracy and its obsession with credentials and collective thinking. A man with no college education, he rose literally from the ranks, made his career in the company that first hired him, and made a specialty of saving faltering stores. More importantly, he clearly loved selling things and discovering ways to do it. As Sears' vice president of retail merchandising, he decided that the one thing the public was clamoring for was an automotive battery that required no maintenance and didn't fail in the winter; he immediately had one developed exclusively for Sears. He would have been a man after old Bill Grant's heart: he identified a market, and he sold things to it. And at W. T. Grant—what W. T. Grant had become—he faced the challenge of his life.

Almost immediately he cut out the big-ticket items, abolished the credit card, and began to shift the stores back to apparel and soft goods, good strategy for the long term but one that considerably worsened the company's short-term prospects. Grant appliances had been marketed under a private label, Bradford, which meant that it maintained its own service centers. With the service centers closed and the service contracts canceled, customers who had purchased their appliances on time no longer felt any great urgency about paying their bills, especially because very few of them had checking accounts and the majority of the cash-payment offices were closed when the credit card was abolished. The bad debts continued to pile up. Meanwhile, the suppliers and the factors continued to balk, interfering with the realignment policy. Buying for the back-to-school season was late and there wasn't enough merchandise; and the supplier problem continued to be bad as Anderson attempted to get the Christmas merchandise flowing through the pipeline.

For a while, it looked as though Anderson might have the time he needed; the small banks took their $56 million and departed, but the big banks stayed with him. It soon became painfully clear, however, that their $600 million wasn't nearly enough. Things didn't get better, they got worse, and the situation was beyond saving. Originally, the loan had required that Grant maintain a minimum net worth of $295 million and $370 million in working capital, figures that were now unrealistic. The banks suspended the requirement. They also subordinated $300 million of their loan to the claims of Grant's vendors, which meant that the vendors and not the banks would have first crack at the company's accounts receivable if it went under. This strategy didn't work. Although Grant claimed to have $300 million in such accounts and $56 million in cash, its bad debts, store closings, and the decline in the economy continued to throw the books out of whack. In September it announced a loss of $111.3 million in the first fiscal half, 500 percent greater than the year before. On September 10, it asked for a 25 percent rent reduction from its landlords. On September 30, it announced that it was operating with a negative net worth, and the SEC suspended trading in its stock.

That did it. The suppliers shut down their shipments altogether. Railroad cars were halted in the yards, trucks were stopped on the highways—and, overnight, business became impossible. On October 2, 1975, with the supplier revolt threatening a total breakdown at the earliest possible moment, the company entered bankruptcy court in New York City and filed for reorganization under Chapter 11 of the law.

Under Chapter 11, a company's management continues in place, attempting to bring order to its affairs while protected from the company's creditors by the court. Grant's creditors were its banks and its suppliers. The remaining banks had already demonstrated a willingness—a foolish, wrongheaded willingness, in the opinion of many observers—to be merciful, extending the surviving $650 million in debt and adjusting the terms as the situation worsened. At bankruptcy, they betrayed a new shrewdness by seizing $90 million in Grant deposits, reducing the loan by that amount, and re-loaning the company $80 million—which, since it was lent after the bankruptcy, thereby became a priority obligation in the event of a final liquidation. Citicorp also wrote off $35 million of its $97 million share of the loan; the Chase and Morgan, each likewise in for $97 million, followed suit.

The suppliers, especially the marginal ones, were simply stuck. With Grant protected by the court, their accounts receivable were immobilized, uncollectible unless the company revived or went under. True, the banks had attempted to encourage them by subordinating that $300 million of the outstanding debt, but for all intents and purposes their money was gone until some new thing happened. Under the circumstances, their choices were two: They could petition the court to change the bankruptcy from Chapter 11 to Chapter 10, whereupon a trustee would try to salvage what he could; or they could help keep the company alive until it worked out its destiny. As might be expected, they did both.

While a committee was formed to petition for Chapter 10, other suppliers decided to give Anderson a crack at running the chain the same way the original W. T. Grant had run his first store, on a strictly cash basis, paying for his goods with certified checks. It wasn't a very wieldy way to run a modern business, but it got the goods flowing again, and it

bought some time. Aware that he now had only months
rather than years to save the situation, Anderson moved with
typical energy. He was running what was basically a cash operation now, a cash operation in an economy based on credit.
As a small blizzard of lawsuits and petitions came in from the
out-of-pocket suppliers—claiming, among other things, that
the banks had lent money to the company while aware that it
was insolvent, perpetuating a species of deception—Anderson
prepared to close 581 stores and return the chain to its old
base in the Northeast, Virginia, and Ohio; everything else was
to be shut down and turned over to the professional liquidators. The surviving core of 493 stores was then to become the
"new Grant," a streamlined and handsomely redecorated
chain selling only merchandise approved from New York
headquarters. New York headquarters itself underwent some
drastic slimming. The staff was cut by about 500 people and
plans were made to abandon the offices at One Astor Plaza—
wryly known as Grant's Tomb—and relocate to less fashion-
able chambers downtown, in space recently vacated by Sears,
Anderson's old company. As a sign of confidence, Anderson
also announced that he was building a new home in New
Jersey.

   A curious situation developed. The suppliers wanted
their money back. Although their liens—that is, their claims
on the company as represented by their past-due bills—were
secured by the $300 million in receivables generously subordi-
nated by the banks, the company was now protected from
these liens by Chapter 11, and the suppliers had to whistle for
it. At the same time, the company had shifted onto a cash
basis, money was coming in from the liquidators, and if you
ignored the balance sheet, things were looking up; in terms of
the more traditional form of money—money the company
could, in effect, jingle in its pocket—the situation began to
improve. But the balance sheet continued to go to hell. Anderson charged all the costs of redecorating the surviving
stores to the current fiscal year, throwing the figures out of

line. Because the payment centers had been closed, it became difficult if not impossible to collect $277 million from Grant's old credit-card holders, further worsening the picture, which was already sufficiently confused by the write-offs and the costs of the wave of closings. Between $75 and $77 million had been set aside in escrow accounts to satisfy the lien holders in states where Chapter 11 protection was insufficiently airtight and was thus unavailable to balance the books. Still, by February 1976, the company was reporting $319 million in cash deposits, as against its estimated working capital requirement of $150 million. The suppliers therefore had a clear vested interest in keeping Grant alive. They were getting paid, the company reported that it had plenty of money, and if the situation continued to improve they had a senior interest in the company's receivables when it came to collecting their overdue bills.

The banks saw the matter differently. Having kept the company alive until it owed a grand total of $110 million to its trade creditors, they were now ready to throw in the towel. One need not look too far to find the reason. They were owed $556 million before the write-offs: $100 million in long-term debt and $456 in short-term. Of this sum, they had subordinated $300 million to the suppliers, but the money was still secured by their junior interest in the receivables and by their unsubordinated interest in Grant's share of its profitable Canadian subsidiary. They had an additional priority claim on the money seized and relent after the bankruptcy, $80 million of it. And Grant now had $319 million in cash, much of it conveniently locked away in their vaults, cash that could be seized to satisfy their outstanding claims.

There would undoubtedly be some problems about that and there would undoubtedly be a real loss, but bookkeeping magic could be used to cushion the blow, provided the bookkeepers were adroit enough. Nobody knew how much of a loss Grant was going to report for the past fiscal year—it seemed that not even Grant knew for sure—but there was no doubt it was going to be considerable. Despite Anderson's reforms, it still wasn't possible for the company or its consultants to generate any meaningful projections concerning its future; after all the uproar of the last year, the company still didn't know how much inventory it had, although it knew it didn't have enough. Possibly that was an improvement, but it wasn't much of one.

Groping and guessing, Grant's consultants estimated that the company might lose around $60 million in the next fiscal year and that it might take another six or eight years to get back on its feet. Armed with these dubious figures—and at the same time, amazingly, requesting a $2.3 million bonus for the liquidators who were closing out the merchandise in the abandoned stores—the company came back with a request for an additional $160 to $200 million in credit. The banks decided it was time to close the whole thing down.

Under Chapter 11, a company's management is allowed to reorganize under the protection of the court, but it must do so with the consent of a committee of its creditors. On February 10, 1976, the creditors' committee appeared before the court and asked for liquidation; the vote had been six to five, with the suppliers in the minority. The court so ruled two days later, and W. T. Grant passed into history, another victim of folly.

Altogether it was a sorry tale from which almost no one, with the possible exception of the belated Anderson and the hapless suppliers, emerges with any honor or a scintilla of moral gravity. That the company's management went mad is perhaps understandable; company managements do that sometimes. In the symmetrical world governed by Adam Smith's invisible hand (or, more accurately, latter-day conservatives' somewhat idyllic version of it), the disease of bankruptcy is soon checked by a shuddering fall, and the world proceeds much as before, a sadder and wiser place where the perpetrators of the act are reduced to the status of beggarmen and ancient mariners. In the case of W. T. Grant, however, the company met with no such sudden and salutary discouragement. It was, instead, positively encouraged to behave like a petri dish of crazed amoebas, thanks to the extension of lines of credit to back its commercial paper. When it then met its inevitable end, it was allowed to thrash around a bit and even to dream of recovery until it built up some cash reserves, whereupon it was slaughtered by its putative saviors. The comedy was only made brighter by the fact that most of this was accomplished by the use of other people's money, including money from the inner cities that Grant and the other suburban chains were in the process of wrecking through their access to Fed Funds.

If the collapse of Grant were an isolated case, one could write it off as the result of an astonishing coincidence—to wit, that the relevant loan officers at upwards of 143 banks were all dozing at the crucial moment, and Grant somehow slipped past them. But what might have been excused as inadvertence in the case of the Penn Central's funding is revealed as a full-blown policy in the case of W. T. Grant, albeit a policy of optimism and neglect of the rudiments of sound fiduciary principles. That it suited the climate of the time is no excuse. The year 1976 was going to be a very bad one indeed.

Before that rude awakening—and before the subsequent meanness of spirit and avarice of intent took hold in the land, as perhaps best exemplified by the administration of Ronald Reagan and the plans of Nelson Bunker Hunt—the bankers would do something else. They would create something very like a gigantic Fed Funds market. They would center it in London, safe from the interference of many of this or any other country's laws. And then, once again, they would go adventuring.

3.

Sadder and Wiser Men: The Bankers and the Euromarket

Banks, like people, believe many things that are untrue. Again like people, they have a way of following policies of proven unworkability, simply because the corporate mind is made up; it is an experience familiar to every child of every parent, and also to the readers of George Santayana. The banks' experience with W. T. Grant and the Penn Central should have demonstrated the necessity of proper research into a borrowing entity and the futility of pouring good money after bad. By the middle of the decade, years of experience with the Fed Funds market should have demonstrated the folly of stripping one segment of society of its cash in order to feed another, rather as if the banks were the foragers of an army; when you behave like that, something is going to happen.

Still, these experiences seemed to suggest nothing to the bankers. Following the flood of OPEC deposits subsequent to the price shock of 1973, the very same multinational banks that had shone so brightly in both the Penn Central and Grant fiascos proceeded to apply precisely the same suicidal methods on a global scale, with some unexpected results. For example, they discovered that countries (like banks and unlike companies that either hum along or slide into gentlemanly oblivion) have a way of behaving rather like people, too. They have policies of their own, and these policies are not necessarily the policies of the banks. And in a world without either colonial empires or a planetary government, there exists no way of making them give loaned money back unless they want to, and no way of tidying up the mess afterward if the worst befalls.

As with the bankruptcies of the Penn Central and Grant, the nature of the trap the banks had conspired in contriving didn't become clear until a startling act occurred. It was another pivotal event in a decade that had seen far, far too many pivotal events; as though blasted by the old Chinese curse, the Western economies were living in interesting times. On November 14, 1979, the U.S. government froze all Iranian assets in American banks, including branches of American banks abroad. On November 21, a banking syndicate led by the Chase Manhattan declared Iran in default on a $500 million loan and moved to seize the Iranian deposits; we shall return to this fascinating event in a later chapter. Still later that month, Morgan Guaranty took steps to attach the Iranian interest in Krupp and the German engineering firm of Deutsche Babcock. It looked, in short, like a lot of bad days and a bloody nose for the wicked Ayatollah and his red-handed fanatics. It was the month we started to take their money away, and high time, too. Then the Europeans started hollering.

On the basis of published news accounts, it was a little hard to understand what, exactly, the Europeans were so steamed up about, but their words, though vague, were strong. The chairman of the second largest bank in West Germany predicted an "avalanche" of claims and a crisis far worse than the one following the collapse of Cologne's Herstatt Bank in 1974. Another European banker stated flatly that further declarations of Iranian default would be horrifying. Credit Suisse accused the American banks—quite correctly, by the way—of violating the unwritten code of international banking.

Nobody outside the banking community had the faintest notion of what they were talking about. They were talking about Eurocurrency and the Euromarket, and they were running very scared indeed. With excellent reason.

Eurocurrency is, in effect, wild money. It has escaped from effective government control. It consists of dollars, yen, marks, francs, sterling, and other currencies deposited in banks outside the country of origin and used by those banks as they use any other deposit, i.e., as a potential source of revenue. If the currency is ever repatriated in the form of, say, a sterling loan to the home office of a British company by the Paris branch of a German bank, the lent money ceases to function as Eurocurrency and reverts to the various controls of its place of origin. Conversely, if dollars on deposit in the London branch of an American bank are lent to Brazil (and quite a lot of them have been), they remain Eurodollars. It is basically very simple: Eurocurrency remains Eurocurrency as long as it never goes home. It is also quite magical. Bankers love it. Largely free from the meddling of governments, it is very profitable, and it grows and grows and grows.

By 1979, when the Iranian crisis threatened, things had gotten so out of hand that if other countries, less impressed than angered or frightened by the bold punitive strokes of the American financial institutions, began calling home their Euromarket deposits, a horrifying thing might indeed happen. If enough countries did that—and if they did it swiftly enough— a terrible secret would be unmasked. In very short order, it would become clear that there was very little real money in the vaults of the titans of international finance, and the whole house of cards might come tumbling down. At the very least, it could be very bad for a very lucrative business.

To place these matters in their proper perspective, it should be understood that the Chase consortium didn't seize money; it seized some numbers on a computer tape. Moreover, the majority of relevant numbers were not safely under lock and key in the homeland, where their seizure would further swell the nation's treasure of digits. Instead, they were under electronic arrest in the Euromarket, which is not so much a place as a thing. It takes its being in the form of impulses shuttling busily from the nerve center in London to Paris to Frankfurt and Rome and Osaka, pausing for a nanosecond on the way to cloak itself in tax advantages at the so-called plaque banks (often little more than a room, a chair, a desk, a computer terminal, and a name on the door) of Luxembourg, Grand Cayman, the Bahamas, Bahrain, and Singapore. It is in many respects a wonderful system, as any international banker will be the first to tell you. In fact, bankers wax positively lyrical on the subject, stressing the market's wondrous speed, its efficiency, its trillion-dollar dimensions, its blissful freedom from the meddling of faceless bureaucrats and the elected servants of the people. Like the Pinkertons, it never sleeps. Somewhere, the sun is always coming up, and the bazaar is always open.

It's all very thrilling, to say nothing of hypnotic, which may do much to explain why the Eurobankers—as they style themselves—appear to have overlooked two rather basic things, one of which they should have picked up in college economics and the other of which they could have learned by consulting a ten-year-old child. The first thing is that the faster you move money around, even in the form of numbers in a computer, the more inflation you eventually cause when the time comes to convert those numbers into cash; by increasing what is called the velocity of money, the bankers in effect devalue their own currency, penalize their depositors, give their borrowers a windfall, and make a mockery of the profit structure of their bank. As for the other thing, the one known by any ten-year-old child, it is this. If you're engaged in handling other people's money, it is advisable to keep some cash lying around, because you may need it.

By contrast with such colorful tales as the demise of the Penn Central and Grant, there are remarkably few startling episodes or arresting individuals in the story of the Euro-market, its evolution, and its blunders; it is a faceless and underpopulated yarn. The market wasn't founded as the result of a bold initiative or a single keen perception; rather, it was something that grew at first gradually and then very fast, a product of the Russians, the corporate boardroom, the well-meaning regulations of the Johnson administration, the cash requirements of multinational enterprises, and the decisions arrived at by some Arabs looking for a bank. No one set out to create a Euromarket, no one planned its development or directed its growth, and its possibilities weren't even properly grasped until relatively late, and then piecemeal, as a variety of interests pursued goals that were not only diverse but also seemingly divergent.

In a sense, then, the story of the Euromarket is the story of money imitating water and seeking a level of profitability in the absence of regulatory restraint, as though in obedience to a natural law. But there is another reason for the relative lack of a human population on the pages that immediately follow, and it is this: a great many bankers either don't understand the Euromarket, pretend not to understand it, or—in rare moments of incaution or candor—prefer not to go on record as admitting that their institutions may have made several tens of billions of dollars' worth of mistakes and, in the process, afflicted the West with a species of inflation that is not susceptible to the usual remedies.

In their public personae, bankers are the most optimistic of God's creatures. When confronted with the possibility that they might have committed a small but telling oversight in compiling their view of the world, they reply that, should the unthinkable ever happen and a giant multinational bank begin to topple, the Federal Reserve will come riding to the rescue like Lochinvar out of the West. So intrenched in the fiduciary mind is this comforting inevitability, so unquestioned is this received wisdom, and so mighty a fortress is the Fed perceived to be that a number of the bankers actually point the naive observer in the direction of the Franklin National Bank, the activities of the Fed on its behalf, and its ultimate collapse. It is the sort of example only a blind man would use.

The Franklin National Bank of New York went broke on October 8, 1974, as a result of huge losses in foreign exchange trading combined with the manipulations of Michele Sindona, the Italian financier and convicted felon. The Franklin was the twentieth largest bank in the country, and its failure was the largest in the nation's history. Many banks were failing then—the crisis years of the mid-1970s witnessed more bank closures than at any time since the Great Depression—but because of the Sindona connection the Franklin is an unusual case and therefore not a part of our study.

It is relevant, though, that its collapse occurred despite the Fed's injection of $1.723 billion in low-interest loans; and it would have collapsed even sooner if the Fed hadn't also been obliged to protect the dollar on the international market by assuming the Franklin's foreign exchange position. Only then was it possible for the European American Bank to purchase the Franklin's assets and assume its remaining liabilities, and the Franklin was allowed to pass quietly out of existence. As the banking community is the first to point out, the depositors didn't lose a cent—and, indeed, the whole adventure looks very tidy. It looks, in fact, exactly the way it's supposed to look, the way it looks in any high school economics text. A bank was tried and found wanting, the Fed intervened, the dollar and the public were protected, and the good guys carried the day.

The real point is that the Fed had a little trouble doing it. Although the invincibility of the Fed is central to the many myths that bankers live by, doling out less than $2 billion to a foundering mid-rank banking institution placed it under a bit of strain. The central bank of the most powerful country on earth flexed its muscles and felt a twinge. It will be well to bear that in mind during the ensuing narrative.

In the late 1960s, the pampered national economy was falling into a slump from which it has yet to recover. The causes of this event are various, but central to the problem was the fact that the country was no longer generating surplus capital. Capitalism's money machine had broken down at the precise moment when the economy was desperate for a massive infusion of cash as it retooled, rebuilt, and stepped up its research and development activities to meet competition from a recovered Europe and a developed postwar Japan. Some of this needed capital was provided by the Fed Funds market, but Fed Funds don't generate capital so much as they move capital around, rewarding corporate giants at the expense of local enterprise, and in the process demonstrating that efficiency in capital movement isn't necessarily the same as good sense. Moreover, the movement of money through the Fed Funds pipeline is only occasionally the redeployment of surplus funds; much of the money in the Fed Funds market is urgently needed at its point of origin, from which it has departed.

To make matters worse, one major response to the new challenge from Europe and Japan had been to export as much business activity as possible and set up shop abroad (in a small but telling example, to manufacture baseballs in Haiti), which, like access to the Fed Funds market, was a recourse that favored large corporations at the expense of small ones. Lyndon Johnson's administration misread the situation and applied classical remedies that only made matters worse. Noting that the export of investment money was creating a deficit in the national capital account that was no longer being made up by a surplus in the export of goods and services, the government implemented a number of regulations designed to lessen the outward flow. Chief among these was the Interest Equalization Tax on foreign stocks acquired and foreign debts incurred by U.S. individuals and corporations, and the Voluntary Credit Restraint Program (VCRP), which put a ceiling on the amount of money that banks physically located in the United States could lend abroad.

On paper, the regulations worked perfectly. The Interest Equalization Tax and related measures effectively discouraged the growing multinationals from repatriating their foreign earnings for later reinvestment abroad, and the VCRP clamped down on the export of capital from the home offices of U.S. banks to foreign individuals and entities. Between 1960 and 1964, parent-bank lending to non-U.S. residents grew at an average annual rate of 22.8 percent; between 1964 (the year of the imposition of the VCRP) and 1972, the annual rate of growth was only 4.5 percent. Unfortunately, these encouraging figures have absolutely nothing to do with reality.

Thanks to three amazing oversights, the remedies imposed in the Johnson years and continued by the Nixon administration worsened the very situation they were attempting to alleviate—and, in fact, did much to create an entirely new situation for which no effective rules have been devised.

The first oversight was to ignore an obvious fact: that if the growing multinationals no longer found it worth their while to repatriate their funds back to the United States, they were going to put them elsewhere. This in turn created an equally obvious need, while threatening the home offices of the U.S. banks with a sizable loss of business. And so, like Willie Sutton, the bankers went to where the money was. In 1960, only eight U.S. banks had foreign branches and their assets came to $3.5 billion. In 1965, responding to changed circumstances, the number of banks with foreign branches had expanded to 118, but because it was still early in the game, the aggregate assets of these branches came to only $9 billion.

A peculiar thing then happened. By the end of 1972, the total assets of the foreign branches reached $90 billion, hardly

an exceptional figure considering the 627 branch offices involved. But by June 1976, the branches' assets had doubled to
$181 billion, a sum equal to 26 percent of the total assets of all
U.S. banks, including those assets held by the approximately
14,000 banks whose activities remained largely domestic. By
the end of 1978, the branches' assets had again almost doubled, to $306.145 billion. This rate of growth is all the more
phenomenal because the credit restraints and the VCRP were
allowed to expire in 1974, thus presumably obviating the need
to retain such vast sums abroad. Nor is this all. Between 1970
and 1975, the international earnings of the thirteen largest
multinational banks rose from $177 to $836 million, while domestic earnings rose from $884 to $918 million. Fully 95 percent of the total increase in earnings posted by the thirteen
largest multinationals came from foreign operations.

   With domestic banking stagnating—and as the decade
wore on, staggering—alongside domestic industry, the competitive advantage seized by the multinationals was immense
and, as we shall see, increasingly perilous. Moreover, some
interesting questions arose as to just how American this handful of banks had become. In 1972, the Bank of America
earned $189 million, 21 percent of which resulted from inter-
national operations; in 1976, earnings reached $336 million,
and the international share represented 40 percent of the
total. Citicorp earned $208 million in 1972, 54 percent of it in
international transactions; in 1976 it earned $405 million, and
the foreign share had risen to 72 percent. The international
earnings of the Chase Manhattan rose from 34 to 78 percent;
of Manufacturers Hanover Trust from 29 to 56 percent; of
Morgan Guaranty from 35 to 53 percent; of Bankers Trust
from 31 to 64 percent; and of Chemical from 14 to 44 percent.

   A couple of things should be borne in mind at this point.
First, a bank's earnings are an imperfect mirror of the scale of
its operations; they accurately reflect only the profitability of
an operation, not its size, and—physically at least—the large
multinational banks remain American if only because most of

the actual banking plant remains in America, as do head offices. For another, money deposited in a bank is not an asset. It is a liability. The money only becomes an asset (and earns profits) when it leaves the premises in the form of an interest-bearing loan. The startling increase in the international-to-domestic profits ratio, therefore, says as much about the condition of the domestic economy as it does about the dynamism of the international money market. The enormous increase in the assets of the foreign branches represents the velocity at which money is being lent and not the amount of money in the coffers.

Unlike the cash in the Fed Funds market, accounting for the origin of all this money is no easy task: $306 billion in international assets could not possibly represent the recycled deposits of the nonrepatriated monies earned by the multinational corporations; $306 billion is roughly three times the annual output of Belgium. In the beginning, between 1964 and 1974, a significant portion of the growth in assets was the result of the second great oversight of the regulators: the VCRP placed a ceiling on foreign lending by U.S. banks located in the United States, but it specifically exempted lending by their foreign branches and subsidiaries. In practice, therefore, the VCRP was all but meaningless; once the foreign branches were in place and the subsidiaries established or purchased, it took but the stroke of a pen (or the punch of a programmer's finger) to move the overseas transactions out of the home office while keeping them within the bank, and the business boomed on.

A compelling but entirely theoretical argument has been advanced that much of the capital starvation that has afflicted domestic business and local government since the early 1970s is due to this continuing shift of funds, transactions, and profits from the home market to abroad. Supporters of this thesis note that the federal government has found itself more and more obliged to intervene with loans to complete the capital requirements of certain projects, such as a department store in Brooklyn or a luxury hotel in Key West, that would have had little difficulty in raising money only a decade ago. The argument is compelling because something very odd is going on when the government has to lend money to a luxury hotel. It is theoretical because nobody has any real idea of what would have happened if the banks had been prevented from moving overseas, because they weren't.

Still, an enormous amount of money remains unaccounted for, even when the VCRP foreign branch loophole is combined with the recycled deposits of the multinational corporations. Only 100 of some 14,000 U.S. banks entered this vastly lucrative international market. Of these, a scant dozen transact the bulk of the business. The business done by this dozen, in turn, is overwhelmingly dominated by six or seven banks, all but one or two of them (depending on the condition of the market) headquartered in New York. Half of the business of this half-dozen is concentrated in two institutions, the California-based Bank of America and New York's Citicorp. These banks continue to receive, respectively, around 50 percent and 70 percent of their earnings from abroad, and the assets of each are approaching $100 billion. That two banks could become so wealthy is in large part a result of the third and gravest oversight committed by the regulators. The regulators had forgotten about the Eurocurrency market.

By a curious turn of fate, the Eurocurrency market was founded by the Russians (with the help of the Chase Manhattan) during the Cold War of the 1950s, when they placed quantities of their dollar holdings in London to ensure that they could not be frozen or otherwise restricted by the United States; like most nations, the Russians use dollars to finance their foreign trade. At a stroke, their prudent action created a deposit of money that the Treasury was obligated to honor but that neither it nor the Federal Reserve could control. The Russian deposit was presently joined by dollars controlled by other sources that had reason to keep them outside the United States, but the market possibilities of the money did not become fully evident until 1958, when the British government prohibited the use of sterling as the financing medium of trade between third-party countries. British banks were naturally anxious to keep this business, and they offered their dollars as a natural substitute. As other European countries placed similar restraints on their currencies during the 1950s and 1960s, the Eurocurrency market was born.

Nobody has any idea of how much money has actually found its way into (or been created by) this market, including the bankers themselves—in the words of one high bank official, any figures constitute "an approximation based on an assumption." The most reliable tables are published by the Bank of International Settlements in Basel, Switzerland, but the figures are subject to many disconcerting qualifications. The computations are based on three primary sources: the World Bank's Debtor Reporting System, the reports of the banks to their regulatory authorities, and advertisements in the newspapers. Unfortunately, only countries that have borrowed from the World Bank are required to report their debts to it, which leaves South Africa and Eastern Europe completely out of the picture. Adding to the problem is the fact that the World Bank excludes debts of less than one year's maturity and debts not guaranteed by the borrower's government, thus excluding all short-term government borrowing, all short-term governmentally guaranteed borrowing, and the entire nonguaranteed international debt of the private sector. The picture is further clouded by the possibility that the reporting government may have no idea of how much money it has actually borrowed. This applies especially to quasi-socialist, military-dominated countries where state-controlled enterprises possess the power to enter the Euromarket on their own, sometimes reporting their debts to the central government and sometimes not, depending on a variety of factors, including the personal relationship between the chief of the borrowing entity and the head of state.

As for the banks that report to their regulatory authorities, many are involved, with many different forms of accounting practices, interior controls, and methods of data collection. Leaving aside the fascinating possibility that some banks, like certain major generals, have no idea of the true state of their international loan exposure, this lack of standardization renders all final figures suspect.

The World Bank attempts to check the data it receives by referring to loan announcements, called tombstones, in the financial press. For a variety of reasons, however, not all international loans are thus boasted of.

Bearing in mind, then, that the Eurocurrency loan picture is underestimated by untold billions of dollars, the gross size of the market—as estimated by Morgan Guaranty—was $890 billion at the end of 1978, 74 percent of it in U.S. dollars. After liabilities (deposits) are deducted from the figure, the market's estimated net size works out to $475 billion, but because accounting practices vary from country to country, bankers prefer to make a further reduction in the total by factoring out loans to central banks and loans to banks outside the market area and by deducting all Eurofunds known to have returned to their domestic markets. This convenient bit of legerdemain then yields a revised net (called net net) figure of $235 billion.

Bankers are sanguine men. They exude confidence and common sense, and like doctors and talmudic scholars they like to give the impression that they are privy to sources of wisdom that are closed to the rest of us. Accordingly, some of them like to point out that in terms of "real" money—that is, money denominated in constant, preinflationary terms based on its value in, say, 1967—the true net value of the Euromarket is only about $100 billion, a trifling sum. It is, of course, very much in the interest of these same bankers to demonstrate that the Euromarket does not exist at all. What all these comforting deductions tend to obscure is that close to a *trillion dollars* has escaped from the direct control of anybody but the bankers themselves. The combined domestic money supply of the seven largest industrial nations is, by contrast, $2.7 trillion. In other words, an enormous hunk of the world's available money—perhaps as much as a third of it—happens to be floating around loose, subject to the conflicting, competitive, secretive policies of a handful of the world's largest banks.

Interestingly, the bankers' assertion of the triviality of the sums may in a sense be true, but not for the reasons the bankers suggest. There really may be almost no actual money in there at all. A huge chunk of this titanic sum of apparent money may be nothing but figures in a computer—fairy gold on an unprecedented scale, but fairy gold that nonetheless is a powerful engine of the world's inflation. To understand how this might be, we have to understand something called the multiplier effect.

According to one line of thinking, a major source of Eurofunds is to be found in the deficit in the U.S. balance of payments, the excess of imports over exports. Aside from the fact that the people who make this argument appear to be looking at the balance of the merchandise trade (automobiles, steel, hot tubs, that sort of thing), where a chronic deficit has long existed, rather than the balance on current account, which includes such invisibles as services and is historically in the black, there are simply no numbers to sustain such reasoning. Milton Friedman has pointed out that although the net sum in the Euromarket in 1969 was a relatively modest $30 billion, U.S. deficits over the previous five years had totaled less than $9 billion. Foreign central banks could have contributed an additional $5 billion from their dollars holdings, leaving at least $16 billion unaccounted for. Even when leakage through the loophole in the VCRP and the dollar holdings of individuals and private companies are taken into account and the various Euroyen, Eurofrancs, Euromarks, and so forth are subtracted, there exists no reasonable external source for these funds, much less for the $475 billion that stood on the books at the end of 1978. In fact, it is possible that there is not that much actual, available cash in the entire world, even with the post-1973 petrodollar deposits of the Arabs taken into consideration.

Admittedly, it is a poser. When questioned on the matter, an official of the Federal Reserve in New York gave an atypically direct answer: "I don't know where it came from," he said. Still, we are dealing with a mystery in the gross vicinity of a trillion dollars, and concealing a trillion dollars is a little like trying to cover a bull with a napkin.

At least a partial explanation of the phenomenal growth of the Euromarket may lie in the electronic nature of modern money and the peculiar nature of a bank asset. Thanks to the miracle of modern telecommunications, it is possible for the Paris branch of an American bank to loan the London branch of another bank any feasible sum of money, and to do so instantly. The money then appears on the books of the London branch as a deposit—a liability that the borrowing bank will immediately seek to convert into an asset in the form of a new loan. Let us say that the money is then moved to yet a third bank in Brazil, where the cycle is repeated: the loan is a deposit, the deposit is a liability, and it must be converted into an asset in the form of yet another loan. Although not one red cent has moved a single inch, a magical growth has occurred in the Euromarket's money supply, which will grow further as the loans are repaid up the chain, creating fresh deposit liabilities that will in turn have to be loaned. So far, so good. Nothing has moved but a series of electrical impulses, and yet the assets of three separate banks have been added to. To those who believe the numbers are cash, this is a miracle of spontaneous generation, but it is a relatively harmless one. As long as the numbers continue to move around in the closed system of the banks' computers, it is all in the nature of a game, and it doesn't matter how fast something moves. The mischief occurs when an entity outside the banks gets hold of some of those selfsame numbers and demands that they be converted into cash.

Up to this point, it's the Fed Funds market all over again, but on a gigantic scale and with the addition of a middleman. As with Fed Funds, money moves from one location to another, untouched by human hands. In the United States, this is accomplished by bank-to-bank transactions, with the deposits of the provinces journeying to the money centers, where they have adventures like the W. T. Grant fiasco. In the Euromarket, the money is first extracted from Japan and the West by means of the price of oil, and the producing countries then place it in the banks, which means that—unlike in the Fed Funds market—the amount of the influx is not regulated by the recipient. Basically, however, the systems do not differ greatly, with one significant exception: the Fed Funds money passes through domestic offices, making it subject to federal regulation, and the Eurocurrency money confines itself to the foreign branches, where no such regulation exists.

Eventually, a certain amount of money must depart from the closed system we have been describing; indeed, the eventual departure of the money is the whole point of the exercise. In the series of transactions we've been following, no money has gone anywhere, but it is about to. In the interest of simplicity, let us say that the Brazilian bank proceeds to make a dollar-denominated loan to a local manufacturer. He won't receive the dollars all at once, of course; they will come to him in increments, after certain conditions are met. Perhaps the money comes from the reserves of the Brazilian bank, perhaps it comes from the stocks of the Brazilian branch of a U.S. bank or from some other source; the point is that some dollars have just appeared in circulation in Brazil. If all goes well, they will be repaid with interest, creating a fresh deposit liability that will in turn be loaned. Remember, something very similar is occurring all along the chain we have described.

Two things are happening here. First, these transactions are being concluded at enormous speed; we are far from the Middle Ages when the great Augsburg banking house of Fugger moved their gold about in bags on muleback. An increase in the velocity of money acts in the same way as an increase in the actual supply of money, and increasing the supply of money is a very good way of causing a certain amount of inflation. Second, there is the miraculous growth that occurs all the way up and down the chain as the money is lent, relent, and repaid, adding to the money on the books of the relevant banks. This new money-on-the-books will, with similarly blinding speed, be converted into money in somebody's pocket, further increasing the world's supply of dollars. And when all of these events are followed to their logical conclusion, there is only one source in the entire world where those bank-generated new dollars can possibly come from: the printing presses of the U.S. Treasury. Here, in vastly simplified terms, one witnesses the multiplier effect. The inevitable result is a certain amount of inflation.

The relevant great banks are not much damaged by the mischief that they do; indeed, it is probable that they aren't damaged in the least. It is a profitable business, a nice piece of change, and one of the main reasons the bankers so dote on the Euromarket. That the multiplier effect is brought into operation as a result of their activities is something they almost never talk about, but this does not mean that they fail to understand it. The multiplier effect has been understood by both bankers and their regulators for a good long while, and the regulators long ago took steps to deal with it. Unfortunately, they did so before the Euromarket came into existence.

When the government created the Federal Reserve in response to the bank failures earlier in this century, it also established a number of admirable rules. One of these is Regulation D, under which all national banks are required to hold between 10 and 22 percent of their funds in reserve against domestic liabilities. This is real money in the sense that it just sits there, earning no interest, and yet it figures prominently on the banks' books and in the strategy of the bankers. The reserve requirement is therefore a way of controlling the domestic money supply and limiting the number of times the same deposit can be reloaned, limiting its potential velocity. In effect, the operation of Regulation D constitutes an effective withdrawal of capital from circulation, and the amount thus withdrawn varies in accordance with the policies of the Fed; it is a flexible instrument. From the lender's point of view, the money has ceased to exist.

The Euromarket is not immune to national monetary policies because it competes with national capital markets, and its interest rates (pegged to LIBOR, the London Interbank Offering Rate) rise and fall in tandem with the more traditional international monies, although money pegged to LIBOR is invariably cheaper. Nor is it entirely unregulated; although England and the other host countries do little but tax the income of the branches (and the bank havens, such as Grand Cayman, the Bahamas, and Singapore don't even do that), the Federal Reserve, the Treasury, and the New York State Banking Department have their men on hand in London. Still, it is a selective oversight.

Although the foreign branches of U.S. banks are parts of corporate entities based in the United States, Regulation D does not apply to them, and the bankers' argument that its imposition would severely impair their competitive position has so far been persuasive, largely because it is true. (In the ideal world of bankers, Regulation D would not exist at all, and the answer of many of them to the competitive threat posed by the Euromarket—including the competitive threat posed by their own branches—is to abolish the rule entirely.) The glories of short-term competition are one thing, however, and the debilitating effects of uncontrollable inflation are quite another. It should come as no great surprise that the years 1972–79, which witnessed a 500 percent increase in the size of the Euromarket and a concomitant increase in its uncontrollable multiplier effect, have also been the years of double-digit inflation in the West. The Euromarket is not the sole villain, but it is one, and to an outside observer it seems absolutely incredible that it should have occurred to no one in power that the nonapplicability of Regulation D might be a good place to start getting things back under control.

(National governments have occasionally tried to intervene. Seven European countries temporarily imposed reserve requirements on the external liabilities of the foreign branches within their borders following the devaluation of the dollar and the abortive currency float of the mid-seventies. There have been other, equally short-lived attempts. Unfortunately, all Western countries are sensitive about the relative competitive positions of their banks vis-à-vis those of their allies, and in the continuing absence of a new international banking convention, any such regulations are likely to remain hesitant, piecemeal, and feeble.)

There are, however, certain limits to spontaneous generation: elementary physics tells us that it is impossible to create something out of nothing. While a good many of the Euromarket's trillion bucks consist of money-on-the-books rather than money-in-the-pocket, the Eurobankers had to start with a nut in the form of some hard cash. In the case of the Euromarket's trillion, the nut arrived in the form of the spoils of OPEC. For the American branches, the crucial factor here was the nonapplicability of Regulation Q.

Until it was disastrously amended in 1980, Regulation Q, like Regulation D, was another of the admirable restraints placed on the velocity of domestic money by a watchful Fed. Before the invention of the Negotiable Order of Withdrawal (or NOW account), it forbade the payment of interest on domestic deposits held less than thirty days, thus placing an effective restraint on money where it moves fastest, in the most mobile deposits. But like Regulation D, Regulation Q did not apply to the foreign branches of U.S. banks. This was extremely fortunate, because short-term, interest-bearing accounts were precisely what the OPEC countries were looking for when the $68 billion windfall came their way in 1974.

Between 1974 and 1978, the gross underestimated size of the Euromarket grew by $515 billion. It is tempting to say that the source of this mighty increase consisted of the spoils of OPEC, and especially the spoils of the wicked Arabs; when it comes to thinking about Arabs these days, a door seems to clang shut in the Western mind, on the surface of which is then projected a little movie of Scrooge McDuck in a burnoose, diving around in three cubic acres of other people's cash. But bear in mind the curious nature of a bank's liabilities and assets. A deposit must be loaned, and while most loans are stable in that they are paid back over a period of time, the Arab deposits have been far more volatile. To be sure, the Arabs have placed a great deal of the money in the Euromarket, much of it through the medium of the American Big Six, and most of that in Bank of America, Citicorp, and the Chase. But they haven't kept it there for very long.

Between 1974 and the end of 1978, the OPEC governments collectively received close to $600 billion, the greatest transfer of planetary capital since Alexander captured the treasury of Persepolis in the fourth century B.C. And they spent it.

Just how they spent it is a matter confused by ignorance and mythology. Contrary to popular belief, the Arabs aren't buying the United States. They haven't even bought New Jersey, although they could probably afford it. The Kuwaiti purchase of Kiawah Island off the Carolina coast notwithstanding, they have exhibited no great fondness for real estate—the British own more of Manhattan than the Arabs own of the whole country. Most OPEC nations don't have any money to invest in the first place; every penny they raise goes for national development and, to a much lesser extent, military hardware. The majority of OPEC countries are simply too poor to export capital, and, for all practical purposes, Saudi Arabia, Kuwait, and the United Arab Emirates (UAE) are the only potential investors on a world scale. But even here, very little has happened. For one thing, they don't have nearly as much money as popular report would have it.

The reason they don't is closely connected with two other myths: the Dracula Theory of international commerce and the Paper Towel Theory of high-absorbent and low-absorbent countries. The Dracula Theory is the more familiar one, and it goes like this: the Arabs have most of the world's oil. Thanks to OPEC, they can charge pretty much what they please for it, and because of the blackness of their hearts, they have imposed a draconian price structure. Japan and the West, compelled to foot the bill in order to keep their videodisc and hot-tub factories humming along, are being bled white.

This is a compelling argument only if you happen to be a barfly. While Abu Dhabi once had a ruler who kept his oil receipts in a box under his bed, those days are gone forever. Not only is $600 billion a highly impractical sum to stash away, but a compelling social need dictated its immediate expenditure. Years of cheap oil had given Saudi Arabia a railroad and Libya a highway and an educational system, but it isn't too much of an exaggeration to say that was it. Vast sums of money generate their own peculiar imperatives, if only because rulers are touchingly fond of retaining their seat upon their thrones and their head upon their shoulders. From the very beginning, the path of the OPEC countries has been remarkably clear: they had to buy as much of a modern economy as they could afford, and they had to buy it fast.

The OPEC price rises created an enormous but highly specialized seller's market. The places where the OPEC countries could buy themselves the infrastructure of a modern economy were remarkably few. They could buy it in Europe, or they could buy it in the United States, or they could buy it in Japan.

Translated into the terms of international trade, this meant that the West and Japan found themselves buying expensive oil rather than cheap oil and making up the difference with a fortune in new exports.

The bankers and their economists knew perfectly well that the return of the money was inevitable, but it was anticipated that the rate of absorption would be uneven. Hence, the Paper Towel Theory. This line of thinking held that while most of the OPEC countries, with their large, poor populations—the so-called high absorbers—would purchase as many capital goods as they could afford, the handful of countries with the bulk of the world's oil would be unable to spend their money anywhere near as fast as they made it, turning them into net repositories. There were sound reasons for thinking so: Kuwait and the UAE were little more than large towns surrounded by oil derricks, while Saudi Arabia was afflicted with a tiny population, a lot of empty sand, and the world's largest oil pool. But while the Arabs, their petroleum, and their cash did indeed go on, as predicted, to become the single great fact of the decade, the Saudis failed to carry out the rest of the scenario.

Between 1974 and 1978, the OPEC countries spent about $500 billion for imports, or approximately 75 percent of their earnings, and these imports grew at an average annual rate of 38 percent. Saudi Arabia's imports, however, grew at an annual rate of 56 percent. By 1978, with a population of between three and seven million people, it accounted for 23 percent of all OPEC imports and was the cartel's biggest spender.

Despite much anguished howling in the capitals of the industrial nations and particularly from Washington, oil prices rose only about 17 percent during this period, and thanks to a combination of slump and conservation (except in the United States), OPEC's world oil sales actually grew by a negligible

1.2 percent a year. Moreover, inflation and price pressures work both ways: petrodollars were worth 19 percent less in 1978 than they were in 1973, and the Western exporters, like merchants everywhere, simply tacked the extra cost of the oil onto the price of their goods.

Inflation, the price squeeze, and the unexpected Saudi expenditures had a profound effect on the overall liquidity of the cartel. In 1973, OPEC ran a surplus in its collective current account of $6.3 billion; in 1974, this sum rose to an alarming $68 billion. But by 1978, the surplus was back down to $12 billion before official transfers and $5 billion afterward; and OPEC's net external assets amounted to less than $170 billion, most of it concentrated in short-term deposits in the Euromarket.

A further word should be said at this point on the subject of oil and inflation. When the price of oil rises, the effects are felt all the way up and down the consumer price index, but a rise in the price of something is not, strictly speaking, inflation. Inflation occurs only when the value of money declines, not when the value of a commodity increases.

As we have seen, an excellent way of causing true inflation is to increase the money supply (or its velocity, which amounts to the same thing) faster than the economy can absorb it. This can be achieved in a number of ways. A government can lose either its head or its nerve and begin printing a reckless amount of money—a thing that happens, but not very often. Inflation can also occur when money that would otherwise be immobilized in conservative investments, such as Treasury bills, is brought into general circulation by such devices as the commercial paper market; the commercial paper market could not, of course, exist without the backing of bank credit. The Fed Funds market similarly but somewhat more selectively inflates the currency by distorting the national loan structure, causing capital starvation in one part of the economy while dumping massive amounts of capital in another sector. As we shall see in another chapter, the banks have also evolved a way of printing their own currency in the form of negotiable certificates of deposit, while the existence of the Euromarket enables them to import fresh funds to keep the inflationary circus going at times when the Fed is trying to tighten the nation's money supply.

And this foiling of the Fed is made possible, in large part, by the vast growth of the Euromarket's electronic money, thanks to a nightmarish combination of the multiplier effect and the short-term deposits of OPEC, particularly of the Saudis—a combination that brings with it not only an indeterminable amount of true inflation, but also bears the seeds of a potential catastrophe.

Once again: to a bank, a deposit is a liability; a loan is an asset. And because of the lack of effective restraints on the Euromarket, money placed there grows at a remarkable rate. In 1973, the Euromarket's assets were underestimated at $140 billion. The important thing to remember is that much of this phenomenal increase was being fueled by the short-term deposits of the OPEC Arabs, unrestrained by the reserve requirements mandatory under Regulation D. These deposits swiftly departed as the Arabs pursued their ambitious development schemes, but they were immediately replenished by fresh short-term deposits and by the interest and principal repayments on the loans they had generated. Thanks to the multiplier effect, the Euromarket grew and grew, and as it swelled, it became progressively more volatile and more fragile.

Because it was heavily dependent on those short-term deposits, its very existence depended on the continued confidence of the Arabs in the international monetary system. If some Islamic potentate were to devise a means of coining his own international currency and therefore lost all reason for using the Euromarket, the whole house of cards could be badly shaken. It is a possibility that bankers once laughed at, speaking disdainfully of worthless pyramids of precious metals in the desert and other such monuments to folly, but in March

1980, it was discovered that a Saudi prince had combined forces with conservative billionaire Bunker Hunt to do just that, by cornering the world's silver. The failure of their attempt nearly triggered a financial panic. Success might have been far worse.

Then, too, in the absence of any reserve requirement, the continuing good health and survival of the market rests entirely with the prudence of the bankers involved in it. Here one might try to take comfort by drawing an analogy between bankers and airline pilots: since neither one of them wants to commit suicide, they will presumably be on the qui vive at all times, diligently monitoring the controls and proceeding with extraordinary caution. The analogy would be a great deal more comforting if the bankers, in their wisdom, hadn't chosen to place fully $93 billion of the market's money in loans to the less-developed countries, or LDCs.

The OPEC prices rises of 1973 and later created a permanent, structural deficit in the foreign accounts of the LDCs. In 1973, their aggregated balance on current account—the combined balance of their trade—was $8.6 billion in the red. In 1974, the deficit rose abruptly to $28 billion. It reached $36.6 billion in 1975, fell to $22 billion in 1977, rose again to $27.5 billion in 1978, and shot through the ceiling following the fresh round of price rises in 1979 and 1980, exceeding $50 billion. Not all of this increase can be laid at the door of OPEC, but most of it can. In 1973-74, the LDCs experienced a commodities boom; this collapsed in 1975, causing an inevitable deterioration in the terms of trade, and the countries have not recovered since. Boom and bust in international markets are familiar phenomena, and tools exist to cope with their consequences—not very good tools, it is true, but with a certain limited effectiveness. A country can usually ride out slack times, all other things remaining equal, and prosperity generally returns to the supplier nations shortly after it returns to the consuming ones.

Oil imports are far less susceptible to traditional methods of restraint, and for nearly a decade oil prices have proven nearly impervious to all cycles but one—an upward spiral. The 1973 rises alone added an estimated $12 billion to the LDCs' annual oil import costs and an additional $25 billion in the form of oil-related increases in the cost of other imports. While the industrial countries as a whole managed to absorb the increases and even make a tidy sum of money in the process, the LDCs found themselves saddled with a permanent annual debt in excess of $25 billion—the price of a fair-sized, endless war.

For the poorest LDCs—those with an annual per capita income of less than $200 and a full billion of the world's population—the situation is grim and worsening toward grave. Few of them participated in the commodities boom, and their growth has been static since 1975. Furthermore, they are not creditworthy, either individually or collectively. The poorest LDCs continue to rely, as they have always done, on concessionary aid from the developed countries, and this aid has not increased, is not increasing, and shows no sign of increasing in the future.

The situation is very different in the handful of LDCs with relatively large, sophisticated, and growing modern economies—Argentina, Brazil, Chile, Colombia, Hong Kong, Malaysia, Mexico, The Philippines, South Korea, Taiwan, and Thailand. Taken together, these nations account for only a quarter of the total population of the LDCs but produce half of their combined gross national product. All have large private as well as public sectors, energetic commercial banking systems, and a growing middle class. Moreover, they are creditworthy. They can borrow money in the open market, particularly in the Euromarket. And thereby hangs a tale.

In the late 1960s and early 1970s, most of these countries found ready access to private credit, as did a few poorer but seemingly attractive prospects such as Indonesia, Turkey, Zaire, and Zambia. For a while the news was very good.

Thanks to the infusion of private funds, their economies grew, and the more their economies grew, the more private funds they were able to obtain. Credit became ever more abundant, old debts got paid off, and the bankers fell into the sort of forever-think that is the besetting sin of their profession; in the teeth of historical precedent, they assumed it would go on indefinitely. Bankers are by no means alone in this optimistic delusion, but they ought to know better. They deal with a very peculiar kind of money, after all, money that is almost never the tangible asset it appears to be on the books. It is, instead, a polite and essential fiction, and the failure of a bank, unlike the failure of a steel company, is a very total thing, not merely because there isn't much to sell off under the sheriff's gavel, but because the money it was supposed to contain simply vanishes.

Bankers have a way of remaining maddeningly confident when confronted with this dread and by no means unprecedent scenario. The source of their confidence is ironically identical with the source of all those onerous regulations they have done so much to escape. Because a bank failure is such an awful thing, it is rendered literally unthinkable (in the sense that alarmingly few people ever bother to think about it) by the fact that the central bank and the central government are empowered to step in and exercise awesome powers of rescue. This bold rescue is predicated on a single interesting assumption: that the central government will be able to afford to do so. As we have seen, recent events suggest otherwise, but as a psychological safety net, the notion of government intervention appears to be absolutely unbeatable, as though it were a promise of immortality signed by God Himself.

Thus equipped, most bankers find it easy to lapse into another of their occupational maladies, called asset hypnosis; it is more than a little like the rapture of the deep that afflicts incautious scuba divers. Because bankers treat loans as assets, they have an odd way of forgetting how much money they've actually loaned, simply because it's all supposed to come back someday, at a profit. They also have an odd way of forgetting how concentrated some of those loans are, both in point of origin and in terms of borrower. In most cases, the thoughts of bankers are the mirror image of the thoughts of the rest of us, but here they try to have it both ways: as far as most bankers are concerned, their assets are as good as money in the bank.

Nothing goes on forever, and sooner or later something like 1973 turns up to spoil the fun. The creditworthy LDCs found themselves in pretty much the same boat as their less fortunate brethren: without significant oil of their own (except for Mexico, Argentina, and Malaysia), without meaningful access to the rich new export market in OPEC (except for Brazil), and without available funds to meet the shocking deficit that had suddenly appeared in their current account. While their outlook was by no means as grim—South Korea and Taiwan made rapid adjustments in their economies and reachieved double-digit growth by 1976, by which time Argentina was also back into surplus on its international accounts—the situation was hardly as rosy as most international bankers and their economists would have us believe. True, the richer Asian LDCs were forging ahead again, variable improvement was made in Latin America, and Brazil and Mexico were able to resume a heartening rate of growth, but a couple of elements were missing from this tidy summary of achievement: the OPEC price rise did not go away, nor was it rendered trivial by the convenient miracle of ongoing economic growth.

The richer LDCs may be vastly better off than the poorer LDCs and their economies may be vastly more sophisticated, but they are still very basic economies nonetheless. Their dynamism is undeniable, but it is based on raw materials, commodities and commodity processing, and labor-intensive cheap manufactures such as textiles. There is no way economies so based can absorb a massive increase in the price of oil unless some external means is found to pay the oil bill. These funds could come only in the form of a massive infusion of new credit, and the credit itself could come only from the Euromarket.

In the past, when a reasonably well-off country found itself falling into deficit, its traditional source of remedy was the International Monetary Fund, which had been established precisely for that purpose. As a member state—and virtually all reasonably well-off, non-Communist countries are member states—it could draw upon the sums it had on deposit as its share of the various quotas the Fund had imposed upon the membership (there have been seven of these levies to date). Under certain very specific circumstances it could also overdraw its account. But while the IMF handsomely fulfilled the purposes of its designers under normal, pre-1973 conditions, there were a number of reasons why it was woefully inadequate when confronted with the consequences of a newly militant OPEC. For one thing, there wasn't enough money in it; at the end of 1979, the Fund's resources stood at $46 billion, whereas the annual oil deficit of the richer LDCs was $20 billion and rising, a figure far in excess of their drawing rights. And like any debt, an IMF loan has to be repaid. Even if the richer LDCs were to avail themselves of their entire quota, inadequate though it is, there is still next year and the year after that.

The existence and purpose of the IMF is based on the notion that a country has fallen into deficit because it has undergone a fall from economic grace and has committed sins. Under a variety of complex formulae, the Fund therefore imposes conditions that the borrower must meet before the money is released, and these remedial measures increase in severity with the size of the loan. A country may be required to raise selected tariffs, particularly on consumer goods, or to abandon subsidies on essential foodstuffs, suspend public-works projects, trim its bureaucracy, raise interest rates, and cut wages.

These are classical remedies, but they have a fatal flaw: they are designed for advanced industrial countries. Even under the best of circumstances, an LDC is likely to find the IMF's conditions draconian if not impossible, as Egypt discovered in 1978 when it allowed the price of food to rise to market levels and found itself with riots on its hands; there is very little give in the economy of an LDC, and none at all in the poorest of them. In any event, the whole question of conditionality is somewhat moot when one is dealing with an oil deficit; oil deficits are caused because oil costs more, not because the importing country's government is a wastrel or unwise.

The IMF's response to the world since 1973 closely resembles that of a man praying for summer in the middle of a blizzard. Although it seemed obvious that one day the world's oil was going to run out and before that it was going to become very, very expensive, the Fund made no preparations for the future. When the price rises came, the Fund acted as though it believed the oil wallahs would shortly come to their senses, abandon their mad schemes for development, and knock the cost of gas back to two bits a gallon. The membership was assessed, a temporary emergency fund was established, the members drew it down, the oil wallahs didn't come to their senses (or lose their minds), and matters remained much as before. As far as the richer LDCs were concerned, the IMF might as well have been broke.

Fortunately, there remained the Euromarket, and the Euromarket had a lot of money. Indeed, the Euromarket had more money than ever before. Although the Arabs never did pile up heaps of cash as they were supposed to—much of the confusion in the world's economy can be traced directly to the fact that the Arabs have done almost nothing they were supposed to do—they were nevertheless running enormous sums through the market's entrepôts in the form of short-term deposits. Furthermore, the banks had already loaned the richer LDCs a good deal of money. True, the amount of these loans paled to insignificance when compared to the amount of money the Eurobankers were about to loan them, but a banker will go to extraordinary lengths to keep from losing an asset, especially an asset in a country that would be doing just fine if it weren't for its oil bill, and in 1974 nobody knew what the hell was going on, how long it would last, or what the outcome would be. It was a new situation, and in new situations, human beings tend to cling to home truths and the principles of past behavior until they either learn differently or are no longer in a position to learn anything at all. In other words, the banks responded to a potential loss by loaning the richer LDCs some oil money.

This is called petrodollar recycling, but in actuality it is nothing of the sort. The Arabs were doing very nicely at recycling their own petrodollars, primarily by spending them in Japan and the West. The Eurobankers only rent them for a while, multiply them in the form of loans, and pass the result down the pike, inflating the world's currencies in the process. All in all, the system appears to work splendidly (if you ignore the inflation, that is). The Arabs retain the use of their money, the industrial countries reap the export dividend and wipe out their oil deficit, growth continues in the richer LDCs, and the banks get rich. Unfortunately, it really doesn't work that way at all.

Since a loan is an asset, a bank emitting many loans has a way of looking terrific—as have those few banks in the Euromarket, where the annual $20 billion in loans and loan rollovers to the LDCs were concentrated. The countries in question are demonstrably solvent, their economies are perking along at a rate more than double the growth in the United States, their productivity is rising, and their reserves are building up in a pleasing fashion. It is all very simple, all very sound, and the only thing wrong with it is that it happens to be a pyramid scam fueled with borrowed money and proceeding with an ignorance of both past history and present fact that is little short of appalling. It's the Penn Central and W. T. Grant all over again, but on a far vaster scale.

The richer LDCs have increased their reserves in the same way they fund everything in the post-OPEC world: with borrowed money. The fact that the money is borrowed means that the assets of the relevant lending institutions are increased. It also strengthens the international posture of the borrowing country. The illusion is almost perfect—and much cited by bankers—until you remember that the money has to be paid back. The foreign reserves of the borrowing countries aren't strengthened in any way; instead, their national solvency is diluted. And the banks are out on a limb until the money returns.

International bankers have a way of regarding democracies as dangerously unstable. Under this pernicious system, Mayor Ed Koch and Governor Jerry Brown and even the Chief of State himself are compelled to return to the hustings once every four years and throw themselves upon the mercy of a fickle electorate. Their economic policies therefore tend to be alarmingly malleable, subject to all sorts of pressures and special pleading, to say nothing of outright threats. From a banker's point of view, strongman regimes are infinitely preferable. Not only are dictators generally charming in their rough fashion, but their plans for their people are often stern, bold, and backed by a powerful secret police; if trouble threatens, they can always shoot a few more people. Adding to the harsh beauty of the system is the fact that it is centrally directed, with the reins gathered in one fist. It is also much easier to understand than a democracy; once you've figured out the character of the leader—usually a simple bloke, though given to the occasional caprice—you've pretty well figured out the government, or you can delude yourself that you have. Lastly, strongman rule is almost always actuarial; not only does the strong man have the populace under control, but he plans to stay around for a long, long time. Strongman regimes bring back the dear, dead days of colonialism, when Lugard ran Uganda and men of his ilk could be found wherever the queen's proud colors flew. International bankers are busy men, and they are properly appreciative of this sort of simplicity, often with strange results.

For example, asset hypnosis combined with the magnetic properties of strongman rule to enable Zaire to obtain more than $400 million in loans. Zaire is rich in copper and other precious minerals, and its president controls many rooms in his palace and several adjacent streets; it is hardly a country at all and becoming less so by the day. Although its actual condition could have been ascertained by means of a few well-placed telephone calls, it did not become apparent to the wizards of finance until the time came for the $400 million to be repaid, when Zaire told its creditors, in effect, to take a walk. Precisely because Zaire is hardly a country, there was remarkably little the bankers could do about this state of affairs. A semi-uncountry is hard to hurt. It doesn't matter much if you block its accounts or place liens on its assets (provided it has any) or threaten never to lend it any money again. In the case of Zaire, the response of the banks was to let matters ride. Short of writing off the $400 million and making an embarrassing admission, there was nothing else to do.

The case of Zaire is instructive, but it is also unusual; most countries in its position could never have gotten the money to begin with. A more pertinent and troubling example of fiduciary bungling is afforded by the Pertamina affair in Indonesia in 1972–76. Indonesia is a strongman state more typical of the richer LDCs and OPEC; it is presumably creditworthy, and it is presumably under control and directed from the center. Unfortunately, countries are not families and dictators are not fathers. In a sophisticated country like Indonesia, there are many centers of power, and of these, the national oil company stood above the rest. Pertamina had money. It also had a chief in the person of a medical doctor and major general named Ibnu Sutowo. Because General Ibnu commanded both the income of a large corporation and the confidence of President Suharto, he was assigned additional development projects, which he brought under Pertamina's umbrella. Because General Ibnu did not, however, have enough money for these projects, he began to borrow some, particularly from smaller U.S. banks eager to get a piece of the international action. Because Pertamina obviously generated an income and because its chief was hand-in-glove with the president, the banks were happy to oblige.

They obliged and obliged, until it became apparent in 1972 that nobody but General Ibnu (and perhaps not even he) had the faintest idea of how much money he had borrowed. It was suspected, however, that the total was dangerously large, and in March of that year Indonesia entered into a one-year standby agreement with the IMF that imposed a ceiling on the country's (and particularly its oil company's) international borrowing.

Banks have recently made much of their qualified enthusiasm for IMF conditionality, but in Indonesia the Fund found itself shouting into a closet. General Ibnu continued to enjoy the confidence of the president, who was therefore presumed to know what General Ibnu was doing. Despite the strenuous efforts of the finance ministry (which the president also presumably monitored), the U.S. embassy (which enjoyed warm relations with the president), and the U.S. State Department (ditto), General Ibnu continued to borrow money and the banks continued to give it to him until Pertamina's debt amounted to $6.5 billion. At just that point, Pertamina ran out of money, and the U.S. embassy began a frantic effort to prevent a cross default that would bring down the company's entire debt structure, rock the country's economy, and possibly have very serious political consequences for friendly General Suharto, who was then defying the Arab embargo and supplying 12 percent of U.S. imports in the aftermath of the Yom Kippur War.

A cross default occurs when, because a company has defaulted on a loan to one creditor, its other creditors invoke a clause in the loan agreement and declare their loans in default too. International bankers scoff at the idea of such a thing occurring, but—perhaps fortunately—the ambassador did not share their confidence. Thanks to the heroic efforts of the embassy staff and the technocrats of the Indonesian finance ministry, the banks were persuaded to sit tight and the story had its usual happy ending, with General Ibnu out on his ear, the debts rescheduled, and the friendly president secure on his throne. Nobody but the banks denies it was a close-run thing.

The Pertamina crisis suggests that the confidence of the Eurobankers in the richer LDCs may be a trifle misplaced. Although it can be argued that the whole sorry episode was the fault of inexperienced, overly ambitious, second-rank banks, the Zaire fiasco indicates that Citibank and the other large multinationals are as capable of flagrant stupidity as the smaller fry. Lest it be forgotten, it was these same multinationals that deemed Turkey deserving of $1 billion in loans. Turkey was not at the time a strongman state, but it was supposed to be another Brazil—an analogy that may prove more exact than its coiners had hoped. Turkey went broke.

When confronted with these and other lending fiascos—the go-go days in Iran, for example—international bankers are quick to remind their questioner that man, and particularly banking man, is perfectable. The principles of the Enlightenment are alive and well in the halls of finance, if nowhere else. "Sadder and wiser men," is how they like to describe themselves, steeped in the wisdom distilled from several billion dollars' worth of mistakes. But it would seem that perfection is a temporary thing. "Wonder boys," says one banker, more candid than most. "About once every seven years we get the wonder boys. They're not like the burglar who plots the perfect crime during his time in the pen; they're like the burglar's son who decides he can avoid all the old man's mistakes. They can't seem to understand that an instinct for the jugular isn't the same thing as knowing what you're doing."

With the exception of Malaysia, a rotating monarchy, and Hong Kong, a colony, the richer LDCs are variants of the strongman model. Brazil is a collegial dictatorship along the lines of a general staff or a board of directors. While Mexico enjoys a lively political life, it is a life legally defined by the boundaries of a single party. The Philippine situation closely resembles that of Indonesia but without a Pertamina, since the Philippines have no significant deposits of oil. They do, however, have a permanent Muslim insurrection, renewed Communist guerrilla activity, and the usual outrageous corruption on the part of the ruling family. Nevertheless, in the 1970s, the sadder and wiser men deemed the Philippines sufficiently creditworthy to support a debt of $3.2 billion to U.S. banks alone. The president of South Korea, where the U.S. bank debt ran in the vicinity of $4 billion, recently met the depressingly commonplace fate of strongmen everywhere. In Chile, President Pinochet has been faithfully following policies of repression and laissez-faire that usually bring about a bank-hating leftist resurgence sooner or later, but the U.S. multinationals nevertheless deemed his junta creditworthy to the tune of $1.7 billion. Peru, which narrowly escaped default in 1976, accounted for another $1.6 billion.

These sums dwindle to insignificance when compared to the top of the line in Mexico and Brazil. In March 1979, Brazil's indebtedness to U.S. banks, the vast majority of it raised in the Euromarket, stood at $14.6 billion. The figure for Mexico was $10.9 billion. Depending on how it is computed, Brazil and Mexico alone accounted for 80 percent of the bank debt of the non-oil-producing LDCs, an enormous concentration. As with all the LDCs, much of it was rolling debt— Mexico's short-term obligations alone have accounted for close to half its outstanding obligations. Although the development projects financed by foreign borrowing earlier in the decade have begun to bear fruit in the form of export earnings, this dividend has been more than canceled by the rising cost of petroleum—it has been obliterated. The debt-service payments of most of the richer LDCs run to around 20 percent of export earnings, an onerous enough burden, but when Euromarket loans by non-U.S. banks are added to the picture, Mexico's debt service runs to around 30 percent of export earnings, and Brazil's has run as high as 40 percent.

Because it sits atop an enormous oil pool, Mexico will escape most if not all of the consequences of this monstrous burden of debt, although it will be interesting to see what happens when the country discovers that a sizable hunk of its new-found wealth is ransomed to a handful of giant banks in New York; oil does strange things to the national psychology. As for Brazil, it happens to be the dry-hole champion of the Western Hemisphere; if it produces little oil, this is not for any lack of a diligent search. In the normal course of events, the IMF would be called in to impose its celebrated conditions, the economy would cool off (provided the populace didn't blow up), and the banks would reschedule the debt in a more realistic manner. The development boom would of course be affected; the IMF's medicine is a harsh one, dependent both on the willingness of the patient and restraint on the part of the oil producers, but it might work. It is also unlikely that it will ever be given a chance. "The Brazilians will call in the IMF," says one economist, "when God is a Brazilian." Indeed, persistent rumors have begun to circulate that the banks have begun to arrange clandestine off-balance-sheet write-offs of the money owed, which—if true—means that the money has simply been lost. And in 1980, the oil bill doubled again.

The situation is very fragile. At the end of the seventies, the richer LDC's owed the Euromarket in the vicinity of $25 billion. By far the greatest proportion of this sum was owed by a handful of relatively prosperous dictatorships in Asia and Latin America, and over three-quarters of *that* money was owed by just two countries, Mexico and Brazil, with Brazil skidding ever closer to default. The money, in turn, was lent by a handful of banks in the Euromarket, about half of them American, which sometimes seemed to know what they were doing and at other times appeared to be conducting their business on another planet. This tiny cadre of banks also happens to be the Arab oil states' preferred place of deposit, and of the American banks, two of them—Bank of America and Citicorp—do the lion's share of the business.

Because there is no reserve requirement in the Euromarket, the money manipulated by these banks is even more unreal than money in a national banking system. It is also very profitable, accounting for more than half the total earnings of the six largest U.S. banks, and the banks have therefore been encouraged to build up the paper side of the market until its gross size stands somewhere in the vicinity of a trillion dollars.

Its inflationary aspects aside, it should be obvious that this mighty fiduciary perpetual motion machine holds the entire economies of Japan and the West to ransom, and its continued functioning depends on the smooth intermeshing of three highly volatile elements: the skills of the bankers themselves, the continued goodwill of the Arab depositors, and the continued ability of the richer LDCs—and particularly Brazil—to roll their loans. But the precedents of the Penn Central and Grant are not encouraging. Under the circumstances, it isn't in the least difficult to imagine a catastrophe of unprecedented magnitude. Indeed, the wonder is that it has worked as well as it has for as long as it has. It only took a single day for the stock market to crash in 1929.

Confronted with this possibility, the bankers remain characteristically sanguine. That the Federal Reserve is not omnipotent seems not to have occurred to them. When reminded of the Pertamina crisis, their answer is that the Indonesian government fixed things. When questioned about the dangers of the lack of a reserve requirement, they recommend that the reserve requirement be abandoned everywhere. When reminded that the Euromarket increases the velocity of money in a dangerously inflationary situation, they reply that it does so because it's efficient. When asked about the rolling deficit in the LDCs, they bring up the IMF.

What we actually have here is a giant Ponzi scheme on a global scale. Nobody planned it that way, but there it is. Just as water seeks its own level, money seeks freedom. As Western governments evolved currency controls in the 1960s and 1970s, so there also evolved a mechanism by which the money could escape.

To be successful, a Ponzi scheme relies on a single great condition: the mobility of money as expressed by the concentration of capital and the dispersal of debt. As practiced by an imitator of Charles Ponzi, it means that he persuades a great many people to give him a great deal of money, handsomely repaying a few of them to inspire confidence, and rewarding the rest with dribs and drabs to suggest future earnings. As practiced by a bank, it consists of accepting deposits, lending them to qualified borrowers, and then relending the same money to other qualified borrowers, thereby increasing the principal and interest payments while diminishing the amount of real money in the system. As long as the system continues to expand, everything works. The charlatan attracts a few more suckers, skins off his take, and makes a few more payouts; the bank attracts fresh deposits, expands its portfolio with more loans, and reaps a profit in the form of interest.

Charlatans and banking systems are subject to two threats, both of them fatal: panic and concentration of debt. Usually the one leads to the other, with concentration of debt coming first: either too much money is extracted from a single sucker, or too much money is lent to a potential deadbeat.

The profound unwisdom of either course is ridiculously obvious; unfortunately, they also happen to be irresistible. The end is always the same: flight or jail for the crook, curtains for the bank.

The Euromarket's capital is concentrated; a few banks do a lion's share of the business. The debt generated by this capital is dispersed throughout the industrial world, the richer LDCs, and a few hot properties like Turkey and Zaire. Following the rise in the price of oil in 1973, however, certain debts exhibited an increasingly unhealthy concentration, and of these debts, by far the greater part was further concentrated in two countries, one of them with no oil. A further concentration occurred on the liability side of the ledger, in the form of short-term OPEC deposits, particularly the short-term deposits of Saudi Arabia, Kuwait, and the UAE—and in the case of one bank, the Chase Manhattan, of the shah's Iran. These deposits, combined with the OPEC-related deposits of the industrial multinationals, provided much of the fuel that funded (and continues to fund) the LDCs' rolling debt.

As they entered the second half of the decade of the seventies, the great Eurobanks therefore found themselves in a position of unenviable and dangerous subservience to their greatest depositors and their least stable major debtors. On the one hand, they couldn't write off the debt of the richer LDCs, the richer LDCs couldn't pay it, and as the resulting rollover proceeded, the debt grew larger—and larger still when OPEC raised its prices again at the beginning of the eighties. On the other hand, the great banks' very survival was increasingly dependent on an uninterrupted flow of petrodollars, a situation that threatened to put the banks in a position of economic vassalage to their own major depositors.

When this unhappy situation was combined with the world financial crisis of 1974–76, it became increasingly clear that a single spark could set off the entire tinderbox. And so it was that the Chase Manhattan, having gotten itself into some perfectly beautiful trouble in 1976, and having almost gotten out of it by 1979, suddenly found itself confronted with a dramatic change in the persona of one of its greatest depositors, and David Rockefeller became a man with a problem.

4.

Mr. Rockefeller's Bank Takes a Bath

It was, as they say, a sobering experience; even the weather cooperated. Thursday, October 12, 1972, was dark and overcast in New York, with a cold rain falling. Just before noon the calls began to go out to the financial press from the public relations desk at the Chase: something was going to happen at 3:30 P.M. Just what that something was, the PR people did not say, but there had been a certain inelegant odor of decay hanging over the bank for some time, and the financial writers didn't have to be summoned twice: they grabbed their raingear and headed downtown. By 3:20 the big boardroom at One Chase Plaza was full. At 3:30, David Rockefeller and Willard A. Butcher, his vice chairman for planning and diversification, came across the threshold and made their announcement. It was short and ugly. Herbert A. Patterson, president of the bank since 1969, had just been fired. Butcher was his replacement.

Patterson was fired for a reason that was not easily discernible at the time. The Chase, the mighty Chase Manhattan, the bank that stood for better or worse in the minds of many as the epitome of American capitalism, the Rockefeller bank—the Chase was slipping. That its relative position had dwindled was, of course, common knowledge; from the largest bank in the nation, it had become merely the largest bank in New York, and now it was only the second largest bank in New York. Whether this was regrettable or a cause for glad rejoicing depended largely on how one felt about the bank's chairman of the board and chief executive officer, David Rockefeller, but in itself it was no great cause for alarm. The Chase was still immense, it was still growing, and if it was growing more slowly than Bank of America and Citibank— well, these things happen.

Insiders and some members of the financial press knew that there was more to the story than that, however. In the few short years since Rockefeller had assumed sole command, the institution had become progressively disorganized and de-moralized. Talented officers were leaving, basic bookkeeping was growing sloppy, and the competitive edge was seriously dulled. The spark had gone out of the place, and it was coast-ing. More interesting is what the insiders and the financial press did *not* know, and what many of them have not realized to this day. The problems at the Chase were more than mat-ters of bookkeeping, leadership, and morale; they were prob-lems endemic to the entire American banking system and the colossal mountain of debt the system had been slowly and de-liberately building since the end of World War II. It was an increasingly shaky structure, not unlike one of those breath-taking inverted human pyramids the Flying Wallendas used to construct on the high wire—and the man on the bottom had just gotten the hiccups. The man on the bottom was the Chase Manhattan.

Patterson's firing was, said *Business Week* at the time, "a stunning move by Rockefeller—indeed a brutal one by the standards of big business and big banks, where discarded top managers are allowed to gently fade away," but it was nothing new to the Rockefellers. As long ago as 1933, Uncle Win-throp Aldrich polished up the bank's tarnished image and strengthened its connection to the Roosevelt administration by turning former Chase chairman Albert Wiggin into a scapegoat for the sins of the 1920s, neatly drawing away the fire of an enraged Congress. The hapless Patterson was just another victim of fate.

It was never clear what Patterson was supposed to have done, precisely, because it was never clear what Patterson *could* have done during his brief, unhappy tenure. He became president in 1969, when George Champion, an experienced commercial banker, reached mandatory retirement age and withdrew as chairman and co-chief executive officer. Rockefeller then took the chairmanship as his own and, more importantly, assumed full responsibility as CEO. Previously there had always been someone up there who knew how to run a bank—Uncle Winthrop, the durable John J. McCloy, Champion—while David pursued his restless travels ("N. S. Khrushchev and D. Rockefeller had a frank discussion of questions that are of mutual interest," *Pravda* tersely reported when he visited Moscow in 1964), reshaped the skylines of New York and San Francisco with the World Trade and Embarcadero centers, exchanged correspondence with President Kennedy on the nation's tax structure, and presided over the Council on Foreign Relations. "You can't run a commercial bank without a commercial banker," an unnamed competitor was quoted as saying in 1965, "and David has never lent any money. . . . It's a good thing for David to have somebody around who can tell him that some visionary idea he has won't stand up bankingwise." Now David Rockefeller was alone at the top.

In 1969, the Chase was still holding its own in its struggle with Walter Wriston's Citicorp for the number-two spot in American banking; Citi (as First National City had renamed itself when it took advantage of Governor Nelson Rockefeller's friendly new banking laws and turned itself into a holding company) was slightly ahead on assets, and the Chase was slightly ahead on deposits. (The Bank of America, nourished by California's even friendlier banking laws and carrying on the populist traditions of its bank-hating immigrant founder, A. P. Giannini, had long ago taken an unshakable grip on first place.) Thanks largely to Champion, expansion at the Chase had been steady and mistakes had been few (the most notable of the latter being the Unicard fiasco—the Chase had led the way with its own bank credit card in 1958, had sold it for $9 million to American Express, and had felt compelled to buy it back for $50 million in 1969, with the Bank of America logo on it).

But by 1972, the situation was dramatically different. Under the innovative and hard-driving Walter Wriston, Citibank's assets had reached $41 billion and its deposits stood at $32 billion, contrasted with $27 billion and $26 billion at the Chase. In 1969, Citibank earnings of $109 million edged those of the Chase by 10 percent; by 1972, the gap had widened to 50 percent. And things were getting worse. A week before Patterson was given the gate, the Chase reported a 10 percent dip in its third-quarter profits, while Citicorp scored a 23 percent gain. Somebody had to go, and Rockefeller was clearly not about to fire himself, although it was suggested.

As they gradually emerged, the Chase's problems centered partly on a matter of bad timing—of not being able to figure out what Walter Wriston was up to until he'd already done it, whereupon the Chase attempted to imitate him. For example, Wriston reorganized Citi into what is called the matrix form, grouping bank operations by function rather than geographical area. Rockefeller and Patterson immediately followed suit, but in such a way that executives were severed from big accounts they had nurtured for years. Meanwhile, thanks to a new cost-tightening campaign, these same executives were simultaneously flooded with paperwork. The result was corporate demoralization and a flight of talent—a vice chairman, a lot of vice presidents—to the competition.

Anticipating a change in the law, Wriston began to position himself to enter statewide banking; Rockefeller again followed suit, but later, after his rival had already snapped up the most promising of the available upstate institutions. Sensing the possibilities of the Euromarket, Wriston began expanding his branch operations abroad until they numbered 242 in 1972; the Chase, following as usual, had set up 101 such branches before foreign governments began having second thoughts in the form of new laws that made further expansion difficult.

Rockefeller attempted an end run around Wriston's poaching on what the Chase had always regarded as its unique preserve in foreign parts by buying minority interests in foreign banks, particularly the British Standard & Charter group with its many branches in South Africa. Unfortunately, this was not nearly as good an idea as it seemed, and it was a public relations disaster. For obvious reasons, civil rights groups were not very pleased by the Chase's further penetration into South Africa, especially in view of the fact that the Chase (in partnership with then First National City, which at the time was headed by David's cousin, James Stillman Rockefeller) had rescued the white supremacist regime from a major liquidity crisis following the Sharpeville massacre in 1960. From a business standpoint, a minority interest in a foreign-controlled firm isn't nearly as good as owning your own branch or subsidiary. Standard & Charter owned a branch in California, which meant that the Chase owned a minority interest in a branch in California, which happens to be prohibited by government regulations. The Federal Reserve ordered the bank to divest itself of its interest.

The Chase had always been strong in its correspondence relationships—the services and training that great money-center banks give to the smaller regional banks in exchange for sizable deposits—but in 1972, even this business was slipping, and fourth-ranking Manufacturers Hanover Trust temporarily took over the Chase's lead in the field. The correspondence business was further eroded by the new regional bank holding companies, which formed smaller banks into groupings large enough to perform many services that had previously been available only in the money centers—and which were also large enough to write loans that had previously been referred to the Chase.

These, then—inept reorganization, flight of talent, the Standard & Charter embarrassment, the decay of correspondence relations—were the bank's most visible problems on the memorable day in 1972 when David Rockefeller destroyed Herbert Patterson's career. It was not that the bank appeared to be in any grave peril—a great bank, like any institution, can be hurt, but by the very nature of its business, it is extremely hard to kill; as long as the world economy holds up, there's always more money coming from somewhere—but serious mistakes had been made, and it had slid into a lock on a distant third place that gave every indication of becoming permanent.

While it was possible that Butcher, as president, an aggressive banker in the Champion mold, could hold the ground, David Rockefeller was still the chief executive officer. And despite the fact that the chief executive officer's wife and the family advisors in room 5600 at Rockefeller Center had persuaded him to cut down on his extensive travels and spend more time at the office, it seemed clear that the chief executive officer wasn't paying as much attention to his bank as his stockholders had a right to expect. The Chase held third place, all right, but it held third place in a banking system that was making a complete hash of its responsibilities. In January 1976, four years after Patterson's departure, it was revealed that the Chase Manhattan Bank was on the list of problem banks compiled periodically by the comptroller of the currency. So was Wriston's Citicorp.

The situation had been building for a good long time. For at least twenty-five years, the capital liquidity of American business firms—i.e., the amount of money on hand to pay loans, build inventory, expand the plant, pay salaries and dividends, and keep from going broke—had deteriorated as more

and more companies turned to the banks to supply their financial needs; the horror stories of the Penn Central and Grant
were only the tip of an immense iceberg. Until 1960, the price
of Treasury bills had acted as a restraining force. To repeat a
previous point, a bank needs liabilities in the form of deposits
before it can gain assets in the form of loans. In the late
1950s, the Federal Reserve held the banks at a disadvantage,
limiting their interest payments to 3 percent on long-term deposits, 2½ percent on medium-term deposits, and 1 percent
on the rest, down to the 30-day deposits on which, thanks to
Regulation Q, no interest whatever was paid. Meanwhile,
Treasury bills paid 3 percent across the board. The inevitable
result was that large corporations preferred to park their surplus funds in Treasuries, diminishing the amount of money
banks could lend.

During the recession of 1960, however, the interest of
Treasury bills fell to 2.5 percent, and Walter Wriston saw a
way of drumming up some new business. This was the negotiable certificate of deposit (CD), a high-interest financial instrument, originally issued in denominations ranging upward
from a million dollars and paying between one-quarter and
one-half of a percent above the Treasury rate. While the CDs
were issued in maturities of 30 days and longer—originally,
six months—the beautiful part was that they could be traded
just like the Treasuries. Not to put too fine a point on it,
Wriston's inspiration put the banks back into the business of
printing a form of money, and the resulting business was
good. The banks obtained some lendable cash and the companies received a new form of negotiable instrument. The
danger was that the Fed could close down the operation at
any time, but it was Wriston's plan to make the CDs so important to bank operations that the Fed wouldn't dare. He
won the gamble: between 1962 and 1966, the value of the
CDs issued by the major banks rose from $5.8 billion to $18
billion.

In 1966, Arthur Roth, Michele Sindona's inventive predecessor at the Franklin National, had a terrific idea. The CD rate was then 5.5 percent; the interest ceiling on savings bank deposits was 4.5 percent. It occurred to Roth that he could make money by selling CDs to small depositors, raiding the savings banks rather than end-running the Treasury. That is exactly what he did. He issued his CDs in denominations of $1,000, advertised the offering, and sat back to see what would happen. In a month, he attracted $420 million, mainly at the expense of savings and loan institutions (S & Ls) in California that had been soliciting a great deal of East Coast money by paying higher interest rates and running ads in the New York papers. It was a disaster. S & Ls, unlike commercial banks, carry the bulk of their loans over the long term, and they require heavy depositor support in order to carry on their business. Home building in California began to contract, a major S & L had to be rescued by the Federal Home Loan Bank Board over the Fourth of July weekend, and Congress began to pay some attention. For reasons we will explore presently, the Federal Reserve deploys a much more tender policy in the direction of the large banks than it does in relation to smaller institutions, but it is also responsive to the wishes of the nation's elected representatives on those rare occasions when the latter give outraged indications of understanding high finance. The Fed accordingly killed Roth's CDs. It also held firm when Treasury rates finally rose above the rates on the larger CDs, which effectively (if temporarily) dried up the market, stopped the influx of corporate funds, and caused a major credit crunch when $3.2 billion worth of CDs came due with no fresh money to replace them.

Wriston and Roth's activities would be little more than an interesting footnote for the delectation of specialists and scholars if they hadn't marked the emergence of something large and dangerous. With the introduction of the negotiable certificate of deposit, the country's financial institutions entered into a hectic era of muscular, evangelical banking rather than the old-fashioned, passive, fundamentalist sort that had prevailed for so many years. Instead of merely servicing the economy, they would now proceed to aggressively meddle with it, producing both handsome profits and unhappy consequences. With the introduction of the negotiable CD, the lid was off the jar and something was loose in the room. For one thing, since the issuance of any negotiable instrument is, in effect, the printing of money, the banks had gotten themselves into the domestic inflation business just as, in a few years in the Euromarket, they had managed to do the same thing worldwide in a somewhat different way: they were inflating the money supply. Meanwhile, as Wriston had foreseen, the CDs had become central to the way banks did business. With the new loans thus made possible, American industry continued to run down its capital position and run up its debt exposure, and a kind of Brazilian situation began to develop.

With big businesses increasingly dependent on credit for their continued good health and expansion, they were naturally dependent on the banks to an identical degree. But with the banks similarly dependent on fresh infusions of surplus corporate funds in order to pursue their aggressive new strategy, a deadly symbiosis developed. Since that new strategy hinged on building up the loan portfolio, the loan portfolio soon grew so large that it was difficult to write it down, and any such write-down would adversely affect the health of the newly credit-hungry businesses on whose continued deposits and interest payments the increasingly fragile structure rested. Any such interruption in the inward flow of cash was, therefore, a threat to the entire system—and to the economies of the West—and with the drying up of the CD market in 1966, a major interruption had just occurred. The banks found themselves selling bonds at a loss to meet their lines of credit, and if the recession of 1967 hadn't come to their rescue, the crisis of 1974–76 might have occurred nearly a decade earlier.

It was as though the banks had learned nothing and remembered nothing. The 1967 recession offered more than a breathing space; it was a chance to regroup, to return to the unglamorous old ways that had served so well for so long with such tiny but steady profits, but the bankers had been to the top of the mountain and there was no turning back. The CD experience suggested that banking could be as exciting and lucrative an adventure as Charles Bluhdorn's contemporary conglomerate building, and a new way was found to keep the good times rolling. It was called liability management, and it centered on the Fed Funds market.

At least since the Middle Ages, banks have ordered their affairs by means of asset management. That is, the size of their loan portfolios was dictated by the amount of capital they had on hand. Over the years, they had learned how to lend a single sum of money many times, but prudence and experience (and the reserve requirements of the Fed) imposed certain limits. Subject to various fluctuations, the usual practice was to multiply deposits by a factor of six—that is, every $100 in deposits could generate $600 in loans. In the aftermath of the credit crunch in 1966, however, it occurred to a number of bankers that money could be found to feed the growing corporate hunger if the banks, as well as their customers, went into the business of borrowing money. It does not seem to have occurred to anybody that this might not be a very good idea.

Still, if the banks were to participate fully in the go-go years of the late sixties, asset management was clearly no way to go about it; the traditional methods of raising funds were inadequate when it came to erecting a lofty Matterhorn of debt, and rightly so. An important part of asset management had once been the accumulation of a store of interest-bearing Treasury bonds that could be sold when it was necessary to build up reserves, but except for the federal bond holdings that were required by law as backing for the deposits of the government, this form of liquidity had long since been abandoned. It was also possible to generate capital by the sale of loans, loan participations, and mortgages, but none of these sources of funds were adequate in the new climate of those years, nor were the banks' traditional borrowings at the Fed's discount window. Loans from the Fed must be collateralized, and much tedious paperwork is required to explain just why the bank wants the money in the first place. The Fed may not always be satisfied and the window may not even be open; in an effort to control the money supply, loans through the discount window are rationed.

There was another way, and it was to be found in the Fed Funds market newly revived by the Morgan. As a hard look at the Grant fiasco reveals, the end result of obtaining money in this way was capital starvation in the provinces and a concentration of loans to a relative handful of imposing companies with preferred access to the credit available in the money centers. But because, in the early years of the market, Fed Funds were channeled through the Fed itself, the Fed exerted a a degree of control over their availability, and the bankers wanted none of that. They were after unencumbered money, and lots of it—indeed, much of the fiduciary history of the last two decades can be understood as a struggle on the part of the money-center banks to discover bright new ways of foiling the government's attempt to regulate their activities and control the money supply.

Negotiable CDs, when the market presently revived, were another promising tool of liability management, but the CDs were likewise demonstrably susceptible to governmental shenanigans. Fortunately, another source of money existed, and this money was uncontrolled. It was to be found in the Euromarket.

In 1969, the Fed again raised the interest rate on Treasury bills and precipitated a second and seemingly greater CD crisis. Raising the rate on Treasury bills is a way of shrinking the available money supply, slowing a boom and—it was hoped—curbing an inflation that was beginning to become bothersome, but whose sources were only dimly understood.

The banks were compelled to pay out $12.5 billion in the short space of six months, and it would seem that the desired effect was achieved in the form of a major contraction of credit. Somewhat to the Fed's surprise, however, nothing happened. The banks simply borrowed $13 billion in the Euromarket, and the boom roared on. When the Fed finally understood what was happening, it choked off the flow by slapping on a retroactive reserve requirement, but the damage was done; the runoff had been covered, credit had not contracted, and liability management had won its first great victory—or so it seemed.

Once the banks abandoned their hidebound ways, it seemed as though there was money everywhere. Great sources of somnolent cash existed in the holdings of the insurance companies, endowments, and pension funds, and it seemed a terrible pity that all this money—intended for widows, orphans, the twilight years of working folk, and the education of the leaders of tomorrow—wasn't out there stoking the furnaces of debt. A good way to get at it would be through the sale of commercial paper, but banks were forbidden by law to issue it. No matter. Thanks to the activities of Comptroller James Saxon and Governor Nelson Rockefeller, banks were allowed to form holding companies. The law says nothing about holding companies, and during the 1969 crunch these new entities sold billions of dollars' worth of paper. The proceeds were used to purchase loans from the holding companies' subsidiaries—i.e., the banks—in a paperwork transaction that kept the loans in the company, again thwarted the government, and made a mockery of the spirit of the law.

The Fed again intervened with the imposition of a reserve requirement, the trick became unprofitable, and that, it would seem, was that. But nothing whatever was done about all the other commercial paper floating around the country, backed by lines of bank credit, and the following year, the collapse of the Penn Central would result in a run that, except for the timely intervention of the Fed, could have had incalculable consequences.

They acted as though it could go on forever; not even the $300 million they dropped in the Penn Central collapse taught them a proper lesson. If anything, the Penn Central smash had precisely the opposite effect, with the Fed's effective dampening of the commercial paper crisis only reinforcing its entirely spurious reputation for omnipotence. The early seventies, when so much soured in the country, was a time of rare fiduciary delusion, as though the bankers, intoxicated by their new role as captains of destiny, had developed a drunkard's somewhat exotic notion of objective reality. Liberated from the shackles of prudence by the wonders of liability management, they not only continued to pump up the nation's debt exposure, but they became downright reckless. It is an axiom of the most commonplace financial management that one does not throw good money after bad, and the lesson the Penn Central should have taught was that something had gone rather seriously amiss in the loan department. The railroad's woes were not only enormous but obvious—it was, after all, experiencing operational breakdown—as was the downright recklessness of W. T. Grant, the plight of Brazil, the folly of General Ibnu, and the status of Zaire. The list of salutory experiences is a long one and includes such items as the $600 million that was lent to the Lockheed Corporation (rescued by a federal guarantee of $200 million of the stricken manufacturer's debt), and the $50 million that was poured into Equity Funding, an audacious but not very complicated ripoff of the insurance companies. Sometimes the government came to the rescue and sometimes it didn't (although it came often enough to suggest that the larger the mistake, the more certain the salvation), but with a pair of such productive money machines as Fed Funds and the Euromarket at their command, it seemed that there was no limit to the havoc the bankers could wreak in the nation's economy and the quality of its life.

But there are limits. It is never wise to go to the same well too often, and when the Real Estate Investment Trust boondoggle blew up in the middle of the decade, it couldn't have occurred at a worse time—"or," in the words of one wag, "to a nicer bunch of fellows." Basically, the idea of a REIT is a sound one; it even seemed foolproof. Land is money, unless it happens to be located in Cleveland or the South Bronx, where a certain expertise with gasoline-soaked rags is required before a profit can be turned. Elsewhere, land almost always appreciates in value, and in inflationary times (such as the banks themselves were helping to bring about) it is one of the more secure investments around. Still, it takes money to make an investment, and good land is very expensive; unless the small investor can find a way of pooling his assets with those of like-minded individuals, he is largely frozen out of the best claims. REITs were the obvious answer; they were created by the Real Estate Investment Act of 1960 for the precise purpose of making such pooling possible. Moreover, the profits were tax-exempt, and the small-scale venture capitalist was assured of a full 90 percent of them after the Trust's manager took its cut. Given the presumed expertise and sound advice that such a trust could purchase, it looked like a sure thing.

At first banks were not much interested in REITs, but the great real estate boom of the 1960s combined with their aggressive new posture to cause them to take a second look. And a madness seemed to take them.

There were many ways a bank could get a piece of the action. It could back the commercial paper of a REIT with a line of credit. It could sell its management skills and the fruits of its research department, making a tidy profit. Thanks to the new Bank Holding Company Act, it could even spin off a REIT of its own, and the Chase did just that; its Chase Manhattan Mortgage and Realty was soon the largest in the business, with assets of a billion dollars. Thus stimulated, the REITs took off. By 1973, they were doing 25 percent of all apartment construction in the country, and the Chase was pouring money into Puerto Rico like there was no tomorrow—or, for that matter, no Brooklyn, no Bronx, no Staten Island, Nor was the Chase alone. Before the bank-driven REITs finished blowing perhaps $8 billion, perhaps $16 billion of other people's money, they lined the coasts of Florida with partly finished condominiums of extravagant ugliness and dubious construction. They started shopping centers and malls throughout the South. They released money without inspecting the work, and they received loan repayments from contractors without asking the source of the funds (in some cases, it was another department in the same bank). They designed all-electric buildings at a time when it was clear to everybody else that electricity was going to be ridiculously expensive for the foreseeable future and perhaps forever. Nobody paused to think that Florida was already glutted with condominiums and shopping centers, that Georgia was reaching the saturation point, or that Puerto Rico wasn't exactly the Pearl of the Antilles. The building went on and on.

At the end of 1974, the comptroller of the currency announced that his office had 150 banks under close scrutiny. In the aftermath of Watergate, nobody paid much attention. In 1975, New York City nearly went broke; many of its bonds were held by the Chase, Citi, and the other money-center banks. There were some uncomfortable questions about how these bondholders had allowed the city to paint itself into a corner in the first place, but the questions were lost in the continuing drama of the federal loan guarantees (again), the rescue attempts of the union pension funds, and the shouldering of another burden by the long-suffering citizens of New York, who were already trying to figure out how to pay for the extravagances of Governor Nelson Rockefeller.

In January 1976, the *Washington Post* discovered the meaning of the code name "Victor." It referred to a top-secret list in the office of the comptroller of the currency. On the list were the names of banks that, following recent examination, had been found to be inadequately capitalized, with an increase in loans of dubious value. Among them were Citibank and the Chase Manhattan.

Nor was this all. Fully thirty banks were considered to be in difficulties of various magnitude. There was bad trouble at the Marine Midland of Buffalo and Union Bancorp of Los Angeles. Citibank was in somewhat better shape—in fact, its condition was "excellent, barring a worldwide catastrophe," such as, presumably, the one that was narrowly averted by the Fed when the Franklin National went under two years previously. The Chase's condition was listed as "fair." There was considerable waffling over just what that meant, with one government witness suggesting that it implied a case of the sniffles. Dodging the question, Dr. Arthur Burns, the chairman of the Fed, felt obliged to warn his listeners that "when you cast doubt on the solvency of individual banks you take great risks with the welfare of the banks and their communities."

Unfortunately for Dr. Burns, the comptroller's definition of "fair" was quite specific. It meant that the bank was poorly managed, with insufficient staff and inexperienced people in key positions. It meant the bank had poor interior controls and auditing procedures. It meant there were a large number of clerical errors in certain accounts—in other words, that stupid mistakes were being made at a very basic level: $109 million of the bank's loans were being carried at a loss; $375 million in loans were probably bad; $1.6 billion were substandard; and another $2 billion required "special attention," which is another way of saying that they might go sour, too. As if this wasn't bad enough, there was the ratio of classified (i.e., problem) loans to gross capital funds, including the funds in the loan-loss reserve. The comptroller's safety ceiling is 80 percent. The Chase's ratio was either 66 or 97 percent, depending on who was talking, with the latter figure the more likely. At 97 percent, again according to the comptroller's definition, the bank was "approaching insolvency," and there was therefore a need for "drastic action, such as changes of control, ownership, or management."

David Rockefeller controlled the bank. He was also identified in the popular mind as the owner of the place. As for management, he was chairman of the board and chief executive officer. He was where the buck stopped, and now, it seemed, there weren't many bucks left.

Then the REIT bubble burst. With problem loans piling up, in March 1976 the second largest REIT in the country filed for bankruptcy. Trusts began going bad all over the country and, specifically, at the Chase Manhattan.

Everything seemed to go wrong at once. Faced with a billion-dollar bloodbath in bad real estate loans, the Chase's REIT was deprived of its power to issue commercial paper. Hilliard Farber, senior vice president and head of the bond trading department, was charged by the SEC with overvaluing the bank's bond holdings: specifically, that the Chase's net income for the first six months of 1974 was overstated by approximately $12,435,000 and that the losses in the bond trading account were understated by $27.5 million for the same period. (Farber consented to entry of a permanent injunction against him, without admitting or denying guilt.) This meant that the bank didn't have tens of millions it thought it had.

The bank held $400 million in New York City securities and another $300 million of the obligations Nelson Rockefeller had racked up for New York State. Between 1971 and 1974, the bank's return on assets had fallen from .73 to .55 percent (and would fall yet further, to .33 percent). The loan rollovers had begun in the richer LDCs, which meant that the bank, like many large banks, was in effect lending itself money.

What was to be done? Rockefeller couldn't fire Butcher the way he'd fired Patterson; the Patterson episode hadn't gone down well with his financial compatriots, and there were already some mutterings that the man who ought to get the sack was identical with the man caught holding the bag—that it was time for Rockefeller to fire himself, if it was not, in fact, overdue. But the Chase was not alone in its misery; in 1976 and 1977, more banks would fail than at any time since the Great Depression. Reality finally caught up. At the Chase, Butcher would have to get on with the urgent job of tightening up the management. The loan-loss reserve would have to be increased, further eroding profits, but there was no help for it. Before the year was out, Rockefeller and Butcher would announce a special three-year recovery program designed to restore the bank's profitability and its reputation. The Chase still had room to breathe. Unlike so many tottering or small institutions, it still had a major and reliable source of funds. So long as nothing endangered that source, the recovery program could be made to work, and it appeared that steps had already been taken to render the flow of money as secure as possible.

The OPEC price rise of 1973 was a disaster for the consumer and a tragedy of incalculable magnitude for the underdeveloped countries of the world, but it was quite a nice windfall for a handful of banks, including the Chase. Between 1974 and 1978, OPEC oil revenues totaled in the vicinity of $600 billion. According to popular mythology, the Arabs then proceeded to spend it on American real estate, invest in American companies, accumulate American military hardware, and fritter away the loose change at Monte Carlo. Only the last two of these are correct. The Arabs are neither fools nor small boys on a spree, and the bulk of their money went for development projects within their own borders, with the unexpended balances held in short-term, interest-bearing deposits in the Euromarket. Although Bahrain, Kuwait, and prerevolutionary Iran exhibited ambitions to set themselves up as major fiduciary powers, the Gulf states in general lacked the skills, manpower, and institutions to handle their own money, and like anybody else, they parked it in some banks. The Franklin National bust of 1974, together with the collapse of the Herstatt Bank in Cologne that same year, caused them to reassess their position, but only by way of limiting their depositories; suddenly mistrustful of mid-rank institutions, they began to concentrate their accounts in the largest, most powerful, and presumably soundest banks in the world, especially Citi and the Chase.

Despite the incredible mess the American banking system—and especially the Chase—was in the process of getting itself into, the choice was a logical one. Arabs and Persians don't know any more about the American banking system than most Americans do, the Euromarket branches paid a rate of interest that was unavailable elsewhere, and David Rockefeller had been at pains to win their confidence in the course of his restless junketings. Despite his recent implication that the acquaintance was limited to an occasional nod as they passed each other on the sidewalks of Teheran, he was especially the shah's friend, and Muslims do business in a very personal way. As for the Chase, the money was extremely nice to have, and as the bank slipped deeper and deeper into trouble, it became essential. This may go far to explain some extremely curious behavior on the part of a longtime Rockefeller associate, Secretary of State Henry Kissinger.

In 1974, the Saudis were worried men. Virtually alone among the membership of OPEC, they were deeply concerned about the consequences of their windfall on the stability of the rest of the Third World and the soundness of the international monetary system, and they decided to take steps. With a small population and a culture attuned to scarcity, they were prepared to take a major cut in their share of the spoils if they could get the price of oil back down to a realistic level. Pursuing this goal in August 1974, they proposed to auction off a substantial amount of petroleum.

The Saudi auction wouldn't have returned the price of oil to its artificially low, pre-1973 level, but it would have effected a significant reduction and perhaps have broken the back of the cartel. The other members of OPEC were natu-

rally distressed by the Saudi proposal, and the royal house
was itself divided on the question. Sheik Yamani, the oil minister and originator of the plan, turned to U.S. Ambassador
James Akins for help.

Akins was a respected career diplomat with twenty-two
years of service. Yamani asked him to fly to London in his
official capacity and take the matter of the auction up with
Crown Prince Faud, the senior member of the princely troika
that runs the country. Akins later told the Senate Subcommittee on Multinational Corporations what happened next.

CHIEF SUBCOMMITTEE COUNSEL LEVINSON: Did you request permission of the [State] Department to go to
London and discuss the matter with Prince Faud?

MR. AKINS: Yes.

MR. LEVINSON: What reply did you get?

MR. AKINS: I was turned down.

MR. LEVINSON: Do you know why you were turned
down?

MR. AKINS: No, I don't. The reasons they gave seemed
frivolous.

MR. LEVINSON: Such as the lack of travel funds between
Saudi Arabia and London?

MR. AKINS: That was one of the reasons . . .

MR. LEVINSON: So although urged by Yamani to pursue
the matter with Prince Faud, you were not able to pursue the matter. Did this cause some subsequent inquiry
on the part of Yamani and other Saudis . . . ?

MR. AKINS: Yes. Yamani and several other Saudi officials were, and I think still are, convinced that the

United States is not entirely serious about wanting to bring down world oil prices.

The conscientious Akins persisted. When Kissinger visited Riyadh in late 1974, the Saudis told him they were still eager to reduce prices or at least hold them steady, but there was a problem. Within OPEC they were a minority of one and they needed support, preferably from Iran, where the United States was known to wield considerable influence. Kissinger gave the Saudis (and Akins) the impression that he would attempt to prevail upon the shah when they met in Switzerland the next year. But after the meeting occurred, the Iranians told the baffled Saudis that Kissinger had said precisely the opposite; he had told the shah that the Americans understood why the price of oil had to go up, not down.

SENATOR CHURCH: [The Saudis] must have been baffled because the Secretary of State, when he had an opportunity to object to the high prices in his meeting with the Iranian government, apparently failed to do so.

MR. AKINS: I couldn't say that. He might have done it and the Iranians might have told the Saudis something which was quite untrue.

SENATOR CHURCH: But in any case, the Iranians told the Saudis that he failed to do so.

MR. AKINS: That's right.

SENATOR CHURCH: Did you then report that to the State Department?

MR. AKINS: Yes, I did.

SENATOR CHURCH: And what were you told in reply? Were you told that the Secretary had in fact objected to the higher oil prices or what were you told?

MR. AKINS: No, I was told that they didn't know how the Iranians could have gotten that idea . . .

MR. LEVINSON: Were you told as well, Mr. Ambassador, that you should stop pressing the question of oil prices, that this was becoming increasingly irritable to the Secretary?

MR. AKINS: Yes.

So irritated did Henry Kissinger become with his ambassador's attempt to pursue an urgent goal of U.S. foreign policy that he fired him.

Washington observers, thinking hard about these events, decided that Kissinger's acts of sabotage were in the service of a higher goal of *realpolitik*: to beef up the shah's treasury to the point where he could police the Gulf. No doubt there is a good deal of truth in the interpretation, but it should not be forgotten that 1974–75 were years when the bank controlled by Dr. Kissinger's patron was getting itself into a simply enormous amount of trouble. It needed those OPEC deposits, especially the Iranian ones, and as time went on it needed them more and more badly. At that fascinating point in the Chase's history, almost nothing could have been worse than a successful Saudi initiative to drive down the price of oil and therefore the amount of OPEC money flowing through the computers of the bank. But, as we have seen, Dr. Kissinger saw to it that the Saudis did not succeed, and a more pliable diplomat was installed in Riyadh.

Oil money continued to flow unabated into the bank, and a good thing, too. Not only did deposits continue to decline, but in late 1974 the Consolidated Edison Company, New York City's giant utility, omitted a dividend, and early in 1975 the Federal Power Commission revealed that no fewer than twenty other utility companies were in danger of bankruptcy. Many of these companies were important customers of the Chase, and money had to be found to tide them over. Then the W. T. Grant Company failed, further disrupting the financial markets, Lockheed's management had to be restructured to avoid yet another crash, the REIT crisis began, and the Victor list was published. The sins of liability management and the go-go years were coming home, and in the entire world there existed only one steady and reliable source of new cash: OPEC.

The Chase was not alone in its dependency on this strange new symbiosis—all the great banks had come to depend on it, and the Euromarket owed much of its existence to it—but the mismanaged Chase was in somewhat worse trouble than the other great banks, and it especially relied on the continued flow of Iranian business. Meanwhile, steps were taken. Forty-six marginal domestic branches were phased out, it was impressed on the bank's officers that they ought to drum up some business, and Butcher's energetic management strategies at least gave the impression that something was being done. The LDC loan rollovers gave the appearance of adding to the bank's profits—never mind that much of the profit consisted of borrowed money, some of it borrowed from the Chase itself—and the Chase entered 1979 with every expectation of record profits. That these profits were dependent in a large part on bank operations in the Euromarket that depended on the continued stability of an autocratic foreign potentate and the continued ability of a handful of Third World despotisms to avoid default was a matter that was not discussed.

Having proceeded this far, it might be fair to ask where was the Federal Reserve and what was it doing while this potentially lethal witches' brew was being concocted. The smart answer is that it was right where it always was, sitting on top of the nation's gold supply down at 33 Liberty Street in lower Manhattan. The smart answer is not far wrong; as the country's banking system began to totter in the mid-1970s, the Fed was doing exactly what it had been designed to do when J. P.

Morgan, David's great-uncle William Rockefeller, and his maternal grandfather Senator Nelson Aldrich sketched in its rough outlines at a vacation resort off the Carolinas in 1913.

While the Fed is sometimes thought of as a central bank on the European model—and while the New York Fed made an industrious attempt to behave like one in the 1920s—it actually consists of twelve regional institutions loosely directed by a Board of Governors. In other words, it is a confederation. The reason for such a diffuse setup was to enable the regional Feds to counter the natural tendency of cash to gravitate to the money centers in New York, Chicago, and San Francisco, thus preventing capital starvation in the provinces. And, indeed, until relatively recently the Fed has actually worked something like that at least some of the time, but the existence of twelve regional banks means that giant national banks find their activities subject to fragmented scrutiny.

It had been consistently difficult for the Fed to figure out what the great banks were up to until they did it, and—since each regional Fed sets its own day-to-day policies—harder still to control them. In fact, although the money-center Feds make a great show of activity, it is relatively easy for a giant bank to checkmate their policies, as in the case of the Fed Funds and Euromarket cash flows. The Fed's true purpose is to act as a lender of last resort, to keep the smaller banks in line (and the monetary system therefore stable), and to flatten out the business cycle through its control of Treasury bills and the discount window. Instead of the old cycle of boom and depression, boom and depression, we now have a more manageable one of boom, inflation, recession, boom, and as far as the great banks are concerned we have never really left the days of Morgan.

In practice, the great banks continue to set the nation's economic policy, and the Fed exists to ratify them. Walter Wriston's invention of the negotiable CD meant that any bank could issue them if it could afford to; the Fed only stepped in when things began to get out of hand in California, and then it made the CDs official by choosing to regulate them rather than abolishing them. By allowing its books to be used as a conduit for Fed Funds, it permitted the great banks to circumvent one of its ostensible purposes—to prevent the money centers from getting their hands on local investment money—and by failing to alert Congress to the possible consequences of the Bank Holding Company Act, it allowed whole new areas of banking function to escape its jurisdiction—as, for example, the Real Estate Investment Trusts. By weakly caving in to the great banks' contention that a reserve requirement in the Euromarket would destroy their ability to compete, it makes the Euromarket and the dangerous LDC loans possible. And by covering the activities and tribulations of the banking system with a nearly impenetrable cloak of discretion, it makes it almost impossible for the people's elected representatives to legislate in the field either sensibly or effectively.

The Fed, like the comptroller's office and the Federal Deposit Insurance Corporation, is extremely tender when it comes to the sensibilities of the great banks. All these bodies act in considerable secrecy when they make their examinations and enforce their rules, and they frequently behave as though they wish the public, Congress, and the press would collectively dry up and blow away. In part, this is a matter of simple prudence; knowledge of difficulty within a single bank or, much worse, within the entire system is a dangerous thing, conducive to massive withdrawals, and a run on the banks is the great nightmare of capitalism. At the same time, the mask of secrecy means that the public, Congress, and the press have very little notion of what may be going on (and going wrong) in its banking system, cannot propose corrective legislation until after the fact, cannot protect the deposits, and cannot be warned of impending disaster in time to do anything about it.

The ironic upshot of all this is that the banks remain at

the mercy of their major debtors and depositors. It has always been thus, ever since the first Florentine lent the first ducat to the first Medici, and it has historically been the way a few great families controlled the economic life of even the smallest town. But with the great banks preferring to concentrate debt rather than spread it—again, W. T. Grant is a good example—and with necessity forcing them to rely increasingly on a handful of depositors from the Gulf, the possibility of disruption increased dramatically. David Rockefeller may have possessed a great name and a great personal fortune, but as his bank began to recover from the crisis of 1976 with the help of OPEC, he forgot something. People and countries are perfectly free to put their money into a bank. But they are also perfectly free to take it out.

One of the acknowledged keystones of the Chase's recovery plan resided in the deposits of Mr. Rockefeller's good friend, Mohammad Riza Pahlevi, the shah of Iran. It was the shah who had run up the price of oil in the first place, in 1973, and it was the shah whom the secretary of state had conveniently failed to inform of the Saudi initiative of 1975. Between April 1977 and November 1979, the Iranian central bank ran some $15 billion through the computers of the Chase. It was quite a tidy operation, as such things go. The money from the oil sales moved from the accounts of the U.S. petroleum companies (many of them in the Chase) to the account of the Iranian central bank in the head office at One Chase Plaza, from which it departed to a short-term, interest-bearing account in the London branch; it was a matter of pushing a few buttons, and it was remarkably swift. Although the revolutionary regime that replaced the shah was eager to terminate the relationship, it was difficult to set up an equally efficient substitute, and between February and August of 1979 an additional $6 million flowed smoothly through the Chase's computers. Still, all good things come to an end, and the Ayatollah's men finally began to run down the country's accounts until, by the crucial month of November 1979, the Iranian deposits at the Chase totaled only $443 million; $396 million of it in London, and $253 million of that in the volatile call account.

It should be borne in mind that the Iranians were not abandoning the American banking system. Far from it. While they were running down their account at the Chase, their deposits at the London branch of Bank of America grew to $1.8 billion. There was an additional $659.4 million in Manufacturers Hanover Trust ($243.8 million in New York and $415.6 million in London), $396 million in Citibank, $332 million in Bankers Trust, and various smaller accounts scattered here and there ($87 million at Marine Midland, $85.5 million at Irving Trust, $27 million at Morgan, and others). Moreover, 1,632,918 troy ounces of fine gold were held for the Iranians in the vaults of the New York Fed. The Iranians didn't dislike the American banking system. Because of their collusion, either real or imagined, with the government of the departed shah, it was David Rockefeller and the Chase Manhattan that the revolutionary Iranians disliked. And it appears that Rockefeller and his bank were about to strike back.

It was his last year as chief executive officer at the Chase, the last year of his three-year recovery plan to restore the bank's profitability, and his next-to-last year in the chairmanship. It was also the year he proposed to salvage his reputation as a banker; David Rockefeller had always been a proud man, pleased to be the first member of the family since his grandfather to hold a regular job. Now a bunch of religious fanatics halfway around the world were running down his deposits by hundreds of millions of dollars, with hundreds of millions more at stake. Hundreds of millions in lost deposits meant less money to loan, especially in the vital Euromarket. Less money to loan in the Euromarket meant less money to loan to finance the LDC rollovers—a partly illusory but highly profitable (from a bookkeeping point of view) business that would be lost to the competition. Worse, the Treasury was already laying plans to freeze Iranian assets in the event that

relations deteriorated further, and a freeze under present circumstances would do the Chase no good; the money would
just sit there until things sorted themselves out again, when
the Iranians would undoubtedly take out the rest of it. A way
had to be found to scrub the books, to save what could be
saved.

There was such a way. Between 1976 and 1978, the Iranians took out $3.8 billion in international loans; $500 million
of it was in the form of a seven-year credit syndicated and
managed by the Chase, with the Chase's own participation
standing at $366 million. There was danger here, too; given
the way the Iranians felt about David Rockefeller, the Chase,
and the modern world in general, they might default.

Now return to the other side of the ledger. The Iranians
still had $443 million in the Chase, $292 million of it in the
worrisome demand deposits (the $253 million in London and
another $39 million in New York). If the Iranian deposits
could somehow be used to wipe out the Iranian loan, the
competition would never get them, the hemorrhage would be
stopped, the danger of default removed, the money recovered, and the books balanced. No further costly additions
would have to be made to the loan-loss reserve, no further
funds deposited in the Fed to compensate for lost deposits.
The bank would be spared another possible $800 million loss,
and Mr. Rockefeller's reputation would be secure. The only
problem was to find a way to do it.

In the context of his personal and fiduciary crisis, David
Rockefeller's activities in late 1979 suddenly make a good
deal of sense; otherwise, they don't.

Thanks to the good offices of Robert Armao, formerly of
Nelson Rockefeller's personal staff, and David Rockefeller's
aide, Joseph Reed, the exiled shah had finally come to rest in
Mexico. David Rockefeller and Henry Kissinger, now back
within the family network as a trustee of the Rockefeller
Brothers Fund, had tried to arrange sanctuary for the exiled
monarch in the United States, but the State Department had

turned them down, as well it might; State knew there was a danger of hostages being taken, and a departmental report had urged that additional guards be laid on at the embassy if the shah were ever admitted to the country. Rockefeller and Kissinger, aided by the durable eighty-six-year-old John J. McCloy, now suggested that the shah should fly to New York for medical treatment. Rockefeller flew Dr. Benjamin H. Kean of New York Hospital to Mexico. (Dr. Kean, a specialist in tropical diseases, was chosen because the Mexican physicians suspected that the shah had malaria. Actually, he was suffering from jaundice, a gallstone, and lymphoma.) Dr. Kean recommended that, among a number of options, it was preferable that the shah, a very sick man, be flown to the United States for treatment, despite the fact—which he later acknowledged—that Mexico had the equipment necessary for the monarch's diagnosis and treatment. New York Hospital is heavily endowed by the Rockefeller family.

Without bothering to check on the shah's condition or inquire about the quite splendid medical facilities available in Mexico City, the State Department relented in what proved to be another disaster of the consistently peculiar foreign policy of President James Earl Carter, Jr.

The chronology is interesting. The Iranians began to run down their deposits at the Chase in September 1979. Shortly thereafter, Rockefeller, Kissinger, and McCloy began their new initiative at the State Department. The shah arrived on October 25 and entered Cornell Medical Center. The Iranians reacted as the embassy and the State Department had predicted, and on November 4 the U.S. embassy and the hostages were seized. On November 5, in the normal course of business, the Iranian central bank sent a cable directing the Chase to withdraw $4,052,951.39 from its London account and apply the proceeds to the next installment of its loan. The installment was due November 15. The Chase did nothing. On November 14, Iranian Foreign Minister Bani Sadr suggested at a news conference that Iran might withdraw all of its

funds from U.S. banks. At 4 A.M. on November 15, State
Department officials set the freeze plan in motion, and the
order was signed by the president four hours and ten minutes
later. It extended to Iranian deposits in foreign branches—the
Euromarket money—despite the fact that the Euromarket
had been set up with the help of the Chase to avoid just such
a seizure and that there was some question in international
law whether it was legal. The order also authorized the banks
to use the overseas deposits to pay off any outstanding Iranian
indebtedness at the foreign branches where, as it happened,
Chase's share of the $500 million loan was providentially
located.

The Chase cabled the Iranian central bank that it was
unable to transfer the installment payment because of the
freeze, despite the fact that the transfer order had come ten
days earlier. On November 19, the bank informed the other
members of the syndicate that the loan was in default.

Amid the subsequent wave of seizures, attachments, de-
faults, mutual recriminations, and arcane legal maneuvering,
a salient fact was forgotten: the Iranians ordered the payment
of their regular installment on November 5, from funds that
remained fluid until the morning of November 15, and the
Chase hadn't done it. There is also a curious coincidence. The
Iranian installment was officially due at 10 A.M. on the morning of the 15th. As I mentioned earlier, State Department
officials were roused from bed at four in the morning of that
very day, and the president signed the order at 8:10.

It is an axiom of history that the larger the stage and the
fewer the players, the greater the drama. While this makes
international politics a great deal more streamlined and symmetrical, in the economic sphere it meant that we were back
in the days of the robber barons, with the acts of a few fallible
men dominating the livelihood of millions. In the great but
brief era of unbridled entrepreneurial competition, a handful
of men played at raiding each other's fortunes; in the strange
new world fashioned by a combination of petroleum and the

Euromarket, a similar game could be played by whole countries and a handful of bankers, and the battle between the Iranian revolutionaries and the Chase Manhattan probably will not be the last of it. When capital is dispersed among many hands in many centers, it is resilient, in the sense that any damage is usually localized and confinable. But when vast sums of the world's capital are concentrated in a few hands, the entire system becomes exceedingly fragile, perilously susceptible to the whimsy, the anger, or the stratagems of a few willful men, with the entire economy of the West at ransom.

The Iranians finally got back what was left of their money, the hostages were returned, and the legal profession will doubtless collect many a fat fee over the balance of the century. Meanwhile, a wave of revulsion had swept the Muslim world. The Great Mosque at Mecca had been seized and retaken at an appalling loss of life. The embassies at Tripoli and Islamabad were burned, and two more died. With Islam thus distracted, the Russians had marched into Afghanistan and received hardly a slap on the wrist. And in the silver pits of New York's Commodities Exchange and the Chicago Board of Trade, a pair of American billionaires and a Saudi prince suddenly found themselves impaled on the horns of a dilemma.

5.

Silver Thursday

On July 27, 1979, unaware of the mountain that was about to fall on them, the executives of the Commodity Futures Trading Commission (CFTC)—watchdogs of the public weal, officers of a regulatory agency with the vast resources of the federal government at their command—met to discuss the silver position of William Herbert and Nelson Bunker Hunt. It was enormous. Nevertheless, this fact did not suggest anything to the commissioners.

"It just seems to me," said Commissioner Gartner, "that there are people with a hell of a lot of money and not a lot to do with their time, fiddling around like you and I might play a game of checkers."

"General feeling of the trade is that these are often actions for tax losses," said Commissioner Dunn.

"Could be, I don't know," said Director Mielke.

"I don't know," agreed Commissioner Dunn.

Exactly eight months later, on Silver Thursday, March 27, 1980, the Hunts' game of checkers came to an end. A lion was in the streets. The Hunt brothers had triggered the first great market panic since 1929, and nobody knew what to do. The price of silver dropped $5 an ounce, to $10.80. (In January, it had briefly exceeded $50.) There were rumors that the brothers' principal broker, Bache Halsey Stuart Shields, was going under. The Dow had plunged 25.43 points in wild selling. Bache and Merrill Lynch urged that the market be closed. The CFTC, the Treasury, the Federal Reserve—all that costly and supposedly invincible regulatory structure that had been erected for just such a moment—reacted as though dazed, and there existed no latter-day J. P. Morgan to step confidently forward and set matters to rights. To those who knew or suspected how frail the Western economic system had grown through twenty years of inventive piracy, flagrant mismangement, and mounting debt, it seemed that the bills were falling due at last. The Hunts had gambled on silver. They lost, and for a brief, horrifying moment, it seemed that they were about to drag everybody down with them.

In the beginning, back in 1973, it had seemed like the obvious thing to do. Equipped with the bulk of the petroleum fortune amassed by their father, H. L. Hunt, and sharing his peculiar political views, Bunker and Herbert felt a compelling need to put their money in a safe—indeed, an invincible—place. To the brothers' way of thinking, this involved something more complicated than finding a good bank and stashing their currency in it. Bunker and Herbert didn't believe that money was worth anything anymore: "Any damn fool can run a printing press," Bunker said. Paper money, severed from its relationship with gold by Lyndon Johnson and Richard Nixon, was a snare and a delusion.

The notion seems almost quaint, but there were reasons for believing that it was an idea whose time had come—or, more properly, come again. Although Bunker and Herbert gave no indication of understanding the first thing about the Euromarket or the multiplier effect, they felt the effects of inflation as keenly as anybody, perhaps even more keenly, since its effect on a fortune numbering in the billions is somewhat conspicuous. In a world distracted by electronic money and its mystifying side effects, the Hunts accordingly prepared

to launch a raid from the past. Morgan would have understood at once what they were up to, and so would Daniel
Drew and Jim Fisk and Jay Gould and Henry "the Silent"
Keep, but all those old pirates were dead and gone, and their
knowledge had died with them. When the blow fell, it was
almost as though the robber barons had reached out across
time, and no one in a responsible position had the faintest
idea of how to parry it.

The Hunts needed a store of value, some physical object
they could buy with their worthless paper money, something
they could control and whose value would not depreciate.
Given the extent of the fortune—somewhere between $6 and
$14 billion, by the most reliable estimates—combined with
their obsession for secrecy and the family's long history in oil,
it was a congenial and perhaps inevitable aspiration. Oil itself
was just such a store of value, and they owned a lot of it. But
with U.S. reserves depleted in the last quarter of the twentieth century, the great strikes were bound to occur abroad,
their disposition at the mercy of unreliable foreigners.
Bunker's bonanza in Libya, the Sarir field, had just been ex-
propriated by Colonel Qaddafi for reasons that made no objective sense (Qaddafi was trying to punish the British for
Iran's seizure of the Tunb Islands in the Gulf, and half of
Sarir was owned by British Petroleum; Bunker just got in the
way), and the future elsewhere did not look bright. Oil is a
mobile substance, but only after it emerges from the ground,
and Bunker and Herbert could no longer rely on being able to
control their sources of supply. They needed something that
was not only mobile, but that they could amass in a secure
location. To protect themselves further, they needed to be
capable of dictating its price, rendering themselves impervious
to the sort of monetary inflation generated in part by the uncontrolled multiplication of loans in the Euromarket. Their
father had begun his career as a cardsharp, and he had
founded the fortune by conning another East Texas con man
in the trough of the Great Depression. The old man had

never known that much about conventional business and neither did his sons, but they all knew how to gamble. So Bunker and Herbert decided to take control of the world's silver supply.

On the face of it, it seems crazy, but there were reasons for thinking it could be done. Herbert says he got the idea out of *Silver Profits in the Seventies* by Jerome A. Smith. Perhaps he did; the Hunts have made major moves with less preparation. True, nobody had cornered the market since the Bank of England pulled off the trick in 1717 on the advice of Isaac Newton. In 1919, Chunilal Saraya of the India Specie Bank began a major cornering operation that netted him 26 million ounces by 1913, when the bank went broke and he shot himself. Nobody had even come close since then.

Nevertheless, the attractions were many. Bunker convinced himself that there were historical and biblical reasons why silver ought to be pegged at one-fifth the value of gold, and in 1973, averaging $2.55 an ounce, silver was nowhere near that. Unlike gold, it was not held in massive quantities with unpredictable sales. It was also pleasingly finite and dwindling; unlike gold, it had major industrial uses, particularly in photography and electronics. In 1973, non-Communist mine production—principally in the U.S., Canada, Mexico, Peru, and Australia—totaled 254 million ounces. Secondary supplies from scrap, government sales, coin melts, and exports from the great silver hoard in India— where, thanks to the laws of inheritance, much of the world's silver is tied up in the form of jewelry—added another 175 million ounces, for a total of 429 million ounces. Industrial and government consumption stood at 493 million ounces, for a net shortfall of 64 million ounces, which had to be made up from the stockpiles of private investors. With mine production stable and with no major sales from the U.S. government stockpile since 1970, the price could only go up. Furthermore, if Bunker and Herbert played their cards right, it could be *made* to go up. Unless they blundered, ran out of money, or found themselves trapped by some unforeseen development, the brothers could invent a money machine, and all the money would be in silver.

Futures markets, as a price-fixing mechanism, have been around since the twelfth century, performing a once invaluable service that has recently come to resemble a cross between a cockfight and a crap game. Their historic mission was to ensure that farmers stayed in business, and that the world was thereby fed. Farmers have a problem: unlike cabinetmakers and blacksmiths, the fruit of their labor comes onto the market all at once, in a seasonal lump, and they have to spend the rest of the year growing it. For much of the year, therefore, the farmer is at the mercy of the money lenders, with only his crop as collateral. Unfortunately, that same crop is entirely worthless as collateral unless some way exists to determine approximately what it's going to be worth in the future, at harvest time, Hence, futures markets.

In a futures market, the farmer can contract in the spring to sell his autumn harvest. This is called going short; it is a promise to deliver the crop, at the price agreed on, some months hence. The contract is purchased by a futures commission merchant (FCM) for either his personal account or the account of one of his clients. This is called going long; it is a promise to buy the fall crop. The system is a closed one: for every sale, there must be a purchase. Since the farmer now has a firm sale, he can go to a money lender and put up the contract, which has fixed the price of his harvest, as collateral for a loan to tide him over the months when he has nothing to sell. The banks are similarly made happy, because the risk of a disastrous price fluctuation is transferred to the speculator represented by the futures commission merchant, the collateral remains secure through the life of the loan, and there is every likelihood of getting paid off in the end. I am simplifying, of course; many creative refinements are possible if the farmer is alert, and the possibility of agricultural calamity is by no means diminished. In its purest form, the futures market is a price-fixing and hedging mechanism, and no more.

But what of those charitable fellows, the futures commission merchants and their speculative clients, who have assumed the burden of risk? Needless to say, they're in it for the money, although they almost never see a grain of wheat or ingot of silver or crate of oranges or any of the other commodities they putatively buy and sell—between 90 and 95 percent of the commodities traded on the Commodities Exchange in New York (COMEX) and the Chicago Board of Trade (CBOT) are never delivered to their speculative buyers, although there have been some hilarious mistakes. Farmers go short in wheat (i.e., contract to sell their crop) as a hedge, to enable them to obtain financing while the crop grows; speculators who may have never worn a pair of gumboots in their lives go short (or long) as a bet. A speculator with a short position is wagering that the price will fall in the interval between the contract purchase date and the contract settlement date; a speculator with a long position is betting that the price will rise.

It would seem that we have a loose end here. On settlement day, something has to happen to the contracts, which are agreements to buy and sell specific quantities of a specific commodity that, in most cases, no one has any intention of selling or buying. In the speculators' case, the problem is solved by assuming an offsetting long or short contract that cancels the obligation. The farmer, who is hedging, will sell his crop elsewhere, but he, too has to dispose of his obligation. This is done by handling it back to the FCMs, who then work some rather complicated—and, for the purposes of our story, irrelevant—magic with it, causing it, too, to disappear. In this great game of snakes and ladders, the winner gets the money.

And before the final reckoning, during the life of the contract, the one who guesses correctly also reaps a modest income. To understand how this can be, it is necessary to understand margins and the various ways they can be played.

In futures markets, there are two kinds of margins: initial and variation. Initial margin is a good-faith deposit of an amount determined by the relevant exchange. (Most brokerage houses require an additional deposit as further security.) If the market becomes volatile, another such deposit may have to be made, but in the normal course of business, initial margin is no great sum. In America, a silver contract usually consists of 5,000 ounces. Initial margin, like a down payment, gives the buyer control of the contract, and, unlike securities margin, it is not mingled with the broker's own accounts. In 1973, when the Hunts made their first buys, control of 5,000 ounces of silver could be purchased for about $500.

In addition to initial margin, a deposit, there is something called variation margin, a daily assessment. Each day at the end of business, when the closing price of a commodity is posted, or "marked to market," the losers in that day's speculation must post variation margin equal to the difference between the face value of their contracts and the marked-to-market price. This money then passes through the books of the exchange clearinghouse and ends up in the accounts of the winning speculators. If the market is undergoing a sustained shift, variation margin thereby becomes a money machine for the speculators who have guessed correctly: if the market is moving up, the longs, who have gambled that the price will rise, batten on the shorts; and if the market is moving down, the reverse occurs. This happens every day, of course, but during sustained upward shifts the longs also have the opportunity, which the Hunts seized, of gambling on a pyramid: they can apply their winnings to new long contracts, take delivery, and use the warehouse receipts as collateral on bank loans, which can then be applied to the purchase of new long contracts. Under normal circumstances a pyramid is a mug's game, a foolhardly risk, since the market is bound to break

sooner or later and that way lies destruction. It can only work
if you control the market, or if you know who does and also
know what his strategy is. The Hunts proposed to control the
market.

Basically, the bulk of the world's silver is traded in two
ways in four places. There are large cash markets and small
futures markets in London and Zurich, and there are relatively small cash markets and much larger futures markets in
New York and Chicago. The cash markets would have their
uses, but for the Hunts' purposes, the place to strike was
in futures, at the Commodities Exchange in New York
(COMEX) and the Board of Trade of the City of Chicago
(CBOT). Here again, one sees the peculiar beauty of silver.
The daily price of gold is determined by a handful of men in
the Rothschild offices in London—the "London fix." The
price of silver is determined in the trading pits at COMEX
and CBOT, fluctuating between two invisible barriers—market limit up, the price above which silver cannot rise, and
market limit down, the price below which it cannot fall—that
are established daily by the exchanges' board of directors. A
more flexible system than the one for gold, it was more vul-
nerable to a raid, and it was so incredibly complicated that
there existed a strong likelihood that Congress and the Nosy
Parkers of the press would never figure out what the Hunts
were up to.

Theoretically, market control isn't as difficult as it might
seem. It is estimated that there are between 600 and 800 million ounces of silver in the world. Of this, 139 million ounces
are tied up in the U.S. government stockpile. Consumption
outruns production. According to Dr. Henry Jarecki, the
sometime Hunt associate and former Yale psychologist who
heads the Mocatta Metals Corporation, a determined speculator would need to corner only about 15 or 20 percent of the
supply—about 140 million ounces—to control the price. At
1973 prices, 140 million ounces would cost about $350 million.

As it happens, there are, at any given time, about 140 million ounces of silver in the depositories of COMEX and CBOT. It looked possible.

It looked more than possible. The government regulatory agency, the Commodity Exchange Authority, was expiring. It was replaced in 1974 by the Commodity Futures Trading Commission, but the new agency's powers were weak, its staff was inexperienced, and its commissioners were soon at loggerheads. COMEX and CBOT were also relatively inexperienced in silver—it had been traded on COMEX only since 1963 and on CBOT since 1968—and neither exchange had ever experienced a cornering attempt in the metal. Furthermore, COMEX, the younger, smaller exchange, had gone extensively into silver trading, and it seemed likely that it would welcome major new speculation, at least to begin with. As for the Treasury and the Federal Reserve, "they considered silver just another commodity," wrote CFTC commissioner Read P. Dunn in an April 9, 1980, memorandum. "They showed no particular interest in silver." The conditions seemed right. The Hunts didn't know it, but they had a lot of learning to do.

A successful cornering operation requires a sophisticated knowledge of the market mechanism and the patience of a serpent, but the Hunts, a notoriously impatient clan, had steered clear of major commodities investments ever since the old man had lost his shirt in cotton in the 1920s. The market is dependent on speculation to keep the price curve relatively flat; unless extraordinary circumstances intervene, the more speculators there are in the marketplace, the more orderly the market, and flattening the price curve is the market's only excuse for existence. In order to corner the market, the Hunts had to effect a squeeze—they had to establish a long position of such strength through their control of purchase contracts that other speculators would be driven away, and the surviving shorts would be forced to finance a portion of the Hunt activity through the variation margin. (To say that the market suffered from excessive speculation when it went haywire in late 1979 and early 1980 is therefore nonsense; there wasn't *enough* speculation.) Once a dominant position was thus seized, the Hunts would have to maintain it by buying a proportion of all the new silver that came up for sale, or their own position would be weakened. But while accumulating their hoard, they had to allow the market to continue to function in a reasonably orderly fashion, or they were likely to attract the attention of the dreaded federal government. And they also had to avoid driving the price up so fast that new silver—silver from India, silver from bank vaults, silver from citizens' sideboards and jewelry boxes—was not attracted in sudden and unmanageable quantities. Lastly, they had to monitor world events carefully, since money flees to precious metals in times of crisis—no matter what the price is.

They made every mistake in the book.

The Hunts immediately attracted attention by entering the market with a 20-million-ounce purchase in the December 1973 contract, and attention is something a man planning a corner should desperately avoid in the early phases of his operation. The market immediately shot upward on rumors that a corner was exactly what the Hunts were attempting, until it peaked at a record high of $6.70 an ounce in February 1974— nobody wants to get caught short in the middle of a cornering operation. The Hunts bought and bought, accumulating roughly 50 million ounces—a third of their probable objective—but more silver suddenly began coming onto the market, silver that had to be bought to prevent a downward price break that would foil the projected squeeze; and there was simply too much of it.

The source of this new silver is not hard to find. It was coming from the Banco de Mexico, which unloaded its entire supply. The Hunts were forced to pause.

During this time, the brothers also apparently took physical delivery of another quantity of silver and stashed it in a warehouse in Zurich. According to a colorful story that has

appeared in testimony and in the press, they sponsored a
shooting match among the cowboys at brother-in-law Randy
Kreiling's Circle K Ranch, with the winners riding shotgun on
a secret night flight of three chartered 707s that flew 40 million ounces from LaGuardia Airport to Switzerland. While it
is physically impossible for three 707s to fly 40 million ounces
of anything anywhere on a single trip, certainly something
happened around the middle of 1973. Figures from CBOT are
unavailable, but somebody drew down COMEX's warehouse
supplies from the January figure of 74,918,645 ounces until
there were only 47,497,901 ounces on hand in September—a
highly unusual state of affairs. Maybe the Hunts really did run
a cowboy flight to Zurich—it smacks of the impetuosity and
innocence that mark some of their ventures—but if they did,
they apparently didn't do it again. Such transfers are easily
and routinely effected by what is called an EFP—exchange of
futures for physical—by which means warehouse receipts in
this country are simply exchanged for physical silver on deposit in the foreign warehouse, and not an ingot of silver
needs to move an inch. In the future, when the Hunts transferred silver abroad, they did it with EFPs—at least in their
detectable transactions.

The corner had failed and the Hunts were stopped in
their tracks. The official version of what happened next says
that the Hunts, having established their position, proceeded
to roll it forward (exchange their contracts as they came due
for new contracts in future months) for the next five years,
but it didn't happen in quite that way. Some of their subsequent trading during the quiet interval before the blow-up of
1979–80 resembles a traditional tax straddle rather than a roll
forward—going long and short in alternating contracts to
achieve certain tax advantages. Bunker shorted substantial
quantities in London in 1975, and he shorted an estimated 8
million ounces in early 1976. He and Herbert had other ventures. Still, they had a lot of silver, and it soon occurred to
them that they might do something else with it.

First, though, they bought some sugar, and how they did so offers a rare and telling glimpse into the way the family does business—if that is quite the word for what they do. On October 8, 1974, they received a phone call from an institutional broker named C. Peck Hayne, who said he had a hot prospect. It was Great Western United, a troubled company that refined 25 percent of the beet sugar produced in the United States, and which was then profiting mightily from a huge jump in the price of sugar. The next day, Hayne met with Bunker, Herbert, and Randy Kreiling in the family office. As Hayne expanded on the bright possibilities, Kreiling took five pages of notes, and the meeting ended with the three of them agreeing to go into the deal for $1 million each.

In late October, they finally decided to see what their $3 million had bought, and they dispatched a young attorney named G. Michael Boswell to New York to have a look around. Boswell discovered that the company's management was in disarray. The Hunts and Kreiling were presented with a choice: either risk losing the $3 million, or take over the company. They decided to protect the investment. It took them a month, it cost them $30 million—$15 million of it borrowed from the trust of their mentally disturbed brother Hassie and secured with silver—and when it was over, the Hunts and Kreiling owned 65.7 percent of their first public company. Boswell was dispatched to Great Western's office in Denver as the new executive vice president and chief operating officer.

So now they owned a lot of silver and a sugar company. Anybody who holds huge stocks of a commodity, no matter how valuable it happens to be, is confronted with a dilemma: if he calls attention to himself, as the Hunts had done, it is difficult to sell the stuff. Large sales drive down prices. Word gets around. Other longs begin to unload. The price goes down further, the shorts get rich, and you can take a beating. In fact, you can lose everything. The large-commodities holder needs to do some highly creative thinking if the danger is to be avoided.

In mid-1976, Great Western entered into a five-year contract to buy between 350,000 and 600,000 tons of sugar a year from the Philippine Exchange Company, a deal valued at between $800 million and $1.2 billion. Payment would be in precious metals, particularly silver. A similar 410,000-ton deal was negotiated with Azucarera la Victoria de Panama, and yet another deal was projected in Nicaragua. The Hunts would thereby be able to use their silver as they originally intended, as a substitute for currency, and they also seemed to have found a way to reduce their position. The trick was to prevent the Philippines, Panama, and Nicaragua from turning right around and selling off the silver as soon as they got it, which would again drive down the price. The solution was Saudi oil. The Filipinos and others would take their silver and buy some badly needed petroleum. The Saudis would, presumably, keep the silver. Their silver would not reenter the market, its price would not fall, and as Great Western purchased more silver (from the Hunts themselves, if need be) to buy more sugar, the price would actually rise and keep on rising, making the brothers' stockpile more valuable and generating the important variation payments from the shorts. It seemed foolproof; if it worked, it might get the Hunts' stalled cornering operation back into working order; if it didn't, the long-term span of the contract gave them a mechanism to unload their holdings. The initial installment for the Philippines came to 20 million ounces, and the total deal could have called for as much as 200 million ounces. In the process, the Hunts would get the sugar.

Great Western stood ready for delivery of 20 million ounces of silver, and prospects looked bright. They quickly dimmed and went out when the International Monetary Fund, which had loaned the Philippines quite a lot of money, ruled that the silver could not be counted among the country's natural resources for the purpose of raising fresh capital, and the deal collapsed.

Great Western—renamed HIRCO, for Hunt International Resources Corporation—managed to make a profit by reselling the 20 million ounces, but sugar prices did not recover, the company continued to operate at a loss, and the Hunts' simultaneous activities in the sugar pit at COMEX did not inspire confidence. "Commodities are traded by a small club of merchants," says a source close to the market. "It's all very close, and when newcomers like the Hunts come barreling into the market, bidding up limit for sugar [that is, bidding the ceiling price established for the day's trading], naturally they were going to get hit with sugar from all directions. They had to be losing money. They must have been hemorrhaging money. Nobody bids the limit." It may have been inept and costly, but it was also instructive. It showed that if you bid the limit on a commodity, you could get all of that commodity you could buy.

HIRCO was still a public company; it had to do its business in the open, and the Hunts weren't used to that. It was an altogether unsatisfactory situation, it wasn't getting better, and something would have to be done about it. Before that happened, though, it seemed possible to put HIRCO to another use. They decided to use it to buy the Sunshine Mining Company.

Sunshine owns 57 percent of the nation's largest silver mine, located near Kellogg, Idaho. From a corporate standpoint, it wasn't exactly the most exciting proposition around: even though silver prices had risen from an average of $2.57 an ounce in 1973 to $4.35 in 1976, Sunshine was only netting about a million dollars a year from its mining operations and its fence-making and electronics subsidiaries. On the other hand, it was sitting on top of an estimated 31,380,000 ounces in reserves. Owning a mine would make the Hunts commercial users and free them from many of the limits the exchanges impose on speculators. It would also give them a major say in the supply side of the industry, and the behavior of the supply side was vital if they were planning more than a market coup. If they played their cards right, control of Sunshine could help them achieve a greater goal.

Unfortunately, Sunshine didn't want to be taken over. The battle raged through the spring of 1977, and when it was over, the Hunts' HIRCO owned 28 percent of the stock, with an option to buy the rest at $15 a share, which worked out to $60 million. The trustworthy G. Michael Boswell was installed as president, and matters seemed nicely settled. There are two interpretations of what happened next. The simplest and most obvious says that Boswell turned on his benefactors. The more devious version, privately circulated by a New York broker named Andrew G. Racz, claims that there was, in fact, no split, that Boswell only appeared to turn his coat, and that he secretly continued to collude in the Hunts' titanic scheme, serving as their stalking horse. (Racz continued to circulate his theory until October 1980, when the Hunts employed his firm to divest themselves of their final 317,130 shares in the brokerage house of Bache Halsey Stuart Shields. Racz received a tidy commission for his services, and thereafter fell silent.)

Boswell's actions are not in question. Shortly after taking office, he advised the remaining stockholders that $15 a share was too low a price. He also implied that HIRCO was mismanaging the company. This unprecedented display of independence had the effect of stiffening the stockholders' resolve and rallying them behind their new president. Boswell was able to buy out the Hunts' interest with money loaned by the company, and he sold the shares to a group of Arab investors. He traded more shares to another Middle Eastern investor, Roger Tamraz, in exchange for Tamraz's London brokerage firm, giving Boswell control of a bullion dealer. While this sounds like a typical W. C. Fields deal, where the sucker is persuaded to exchange his house and his car for part ownership in the Lost Bullfrog Mine, it also is exactly what happened. With slight modifications, these were the same moves the Hunts would shortly make on a far grander scale. In February 1980, anticipating his former employers by a month and a half, Boswell tested the international market for a novel bond offering. The bonds were indexed to the price of silver; in effect, they were backed by silver. On a modest scale, they amounted to a private remonitization of the metal. According to sources at Drexel Burnham Lambert, the brokerage handling the deal, the idea had originated with Nelson Bunker Hunt. Whether maverick or mole, it would seem that Boswell was implementing a carefully thought-out plan depending on three elements: control of a bullion dealer, Arab money, and silver bonds. It was on the second of these elements that the entire Hunt plan now swung.

As their knowledge of the market matured, the Hunts had discovered a new problem. They didn't have enough money. The Banco de Mexico sale of silver in 1974 had revealed a fatal flaw in their calculations; as they drove the price up, they could be taken on the flank by a major influx of fresh supplies. In order to prevent their gains from being canceled out—remember, they weren't merely trying to buy silver, they were trying to buy enough to control the world market—they needed some insurance in the form of a massive infusion of fresh capital. Once the market got rolling in a desirably upward direction, much of this money would be provided by a pyramid financed by the squeeze on the shorts, but until then they were going to need more cash, a lot more cash. That meant they were either going to have to take some loans or they were going to have to find some partners. Loans for the requisite amount were dangerous. The requisite amount was huge; in the mid and late 1970s, silver cost around $4 an ounce. If another 50 million ounces appeared out of nowhere, it would take at least $200 million to buy it. It would probably take more than $200 million, and even more—much more—

would be required to move the market. Bank loans would be essential, but they could not provide the needed flexibility. The Hunts needed some allies. There could not be many of them; they would have to be loyal; they would have to be fabulously wealthy; and they would have to have access to large sums of ready cash. In mid-March 1975, Bunker Hunt flew to Teheran.

The shah was unavailable, but the finance minister lent his ear. Bunker outlined his plan. It was very simple. The Iranians would take a month's petroleum revenues and buy some silver—not Hunt silver, but COMEX or CBOT silver or London silver—and store it in Zurich as a hedge against inflation. Pondering this proposal as he eyed Mr. Hunt's cheap Iranian shirt and crumpled clothing, the finance minister asked him how much he had made last year. Bunker's suggestion did not bear fruit.

With his aide (since defected) Bill Bledsoe, Bunker then flew to Europe, dropped Bledsoe off in Zurich, and continued on to Paris to look at his racehorses. Acting on instructions from Herbert, Bledsoe arranged for additional warehouse space for the family silver. He also called on the Union Bank, Credit Suisse, the Swiss Bank Corporation, and the Banque Populaire. Bunker and Herbert were planning to buy an additional 25 or 30 million ounces of silver and they wanted to know if the banks would put up between 75 and 80 percent of the money, with the loans secured by the warehouse receipts on the more than 20 million ounces they physically held in the United States. The banks showed a willingness to oblige.

Bunker next planned to fly to Jidda and lay his proposal before King Faisal, but the monarch was assassinated before the trip could take place. The Arab play was put on hold, but it was still a good idea. The money was there. Arabs traditionally favor investments that offer a high yield, maximum liquidity, and absolute security. Silver would be an attractive proposition. Moreover, Arabs do business in a highly personal way, through family alliances and friendship, and they are loyal—until they come to feel betrayed.

Once again, however, the Hunts were distracted. They finally managed to corner something. In August 1976, it was noticed that the price of soybeans had been undergoing a rather peculiar parallel with the price of silver for the previous four months. No one seemed to know what, if anything, this meant. However, if someone had a massive position in silver, and if that same person had a massive position in soybeans, and if he were moving his positions forward in tandem, identical price curves would result. Soybeans are traded in Chicago. The CBOT is a secretive exchange, which is one of the reasons the Hunts moved the bulk of their silver positions there in 1975. Nothing useful can be discovered about their trading pattern until 1977, when it was revealed that Bunker, Herbert, five of their children, and a family holding company owned 22.7 million bushels out of a national supply of 65 million bushels, and they controlled the market. Houston Hunt, Bunker's eighteen-year-old son, later testified that he made $7.5 million over the pay phone in his fraternity house. The Chicago limit for individual trading is 3 million bushels. The Hunts denied that they were trading in concert; their mutual presence in soybeans was, it seemed, just a big coincidence.

The brazenness of it all was too much even for the CFTC, and for once it reacted. It hauled the boys into court and made them spend money to defend themselves. The result was curious. After much toing and froing, the federal court handed down a preliminary injunction ordering the Hunts to obey the trading limits—in other words, they were instructed to obey the law. But more than a year passed and the injunction was not made permanent. Meanwhile, the CFTC administrative judge carefully reviewed all possible sanctions and, one by one, found them inapplicable. The CFTC then asked the judge to reconsider. As of this writing, no decision has been made.

It was another instructive venture. It demonstrated that you could rob a house and get away with it so long as you claimed you were just passing through. The lesson was not lost.

The Hunts were almost ready to try silver again. Their bungling in sugar had shown them the possibilities of uplimit bidding; it acted like a powerful magnet. The Swiss stood ready with lines of credit. Their experience in soybeans had shown that control was more than theoretically possible. They had also shown that the CFTC couldn't stop a determined operation, position limits or no position limits. But the Hunts still needed partners. Their various speculations were causing recurrent cash shortages at various points in the family empire, and they were presently going to require an almost unimaginable amount of money. It was time to approach the Arabs again.

In the middle and late 1970s, there was a certain amount of worried talk about the possibility of an Arab money weapon that would supplement or perhaps surpass the power of the oil weapon that had been deployed (in the form of a boycott of Israel's supporters) during the Yom Kippur War of 1973. Superficially, the reasoning seemed compelling. Thanks to OPEC, the Arabs had amassed one of the greatest concentrations of capital on the planet. This fortune was the principal motive force behind the incredible expansion of the Euromarket, where, because of the mismanagement and disarray in the domestic American banking system, more than half of the profits of some of the world's most important banks were generated. Given that very mismanagement and disarray (combined with the necessity of continued Brazilian rollovers), the precarious smooth functioning of the Euromarket was essential to the continued survival of the world financial system. Should the Arabs perceive this, they could therefore threaten the world order to achieve some goal or policy, such as the annihilation of Israel, or if they were defied, they could destroy it.

Indeed, something of the sort happened during the Iranian crisis, when the revolutionary government abandoned the Chase Manhattan Bank, but the parallels are not exact. For one thing, the Iranians had been withdrawing their money relatively slowly, giving the government time to react. For another, when the Carter administration did react, it audaciously and perhaps illegally defied the whole notion of the Euromarket by freezing the Iranian funds there—a bold stroke that had not been foreseen.

In practice, the deployment of the money weapon on a grander and swifter scale was made impractical by a number of seemingly invincible constraints. Because their wealth is denominated in currency, the Arabs have a powerful vested interest in preserving the world financial system, not in destroying it; they would pauperize themselves along with everybody else. Then there was the problem of where to put the money once they took it out. Money, like nature, abhors a vacuum. If, say, the Saudis attempted to punish the United States by removing their money and placing it in German depositories, the German depositories would immediately lend or sell it directly back to the Americans, who would understandably be in the market. And since money, like wheat, is a fungible substance (that is, every dollar, like every grain of wheat, is much like every other dollar and becomes anonymous when mingled), there would be no practical way for the Saudis to stop the process—which would also occur instantly. Lastly, the Saudis could take their money and burn it, which would have the desired effect but would also pauperize them, or they could convert it into precious metals.

There was a certain amount of hilarity expressed over this latter option. It was feasible, but it also seemed insane. The purchase of precious metals would only enrich the sellers, returning the money to the system once the sellers had laughed their way to the bank. Moreover, there appeared to be nothing the Arabs could do with their store of precious metals except turn around and sell it again, in which case, like Bunker Hunt, they would be at the none-too-tender mercies of the purchasers, or they could build a pyramid with it, rendering it conspicuous but useless. It occurred to no one that the Arabs might decide to abandon the world monetary system altogether and mint their own currency—a currency backed with precious metals that, given the sort of chaos that had prevailed in the world capital market during the last decade, would suddenly become the most expensive, powerful, and desirable money in the world. And the Hunt brothers were about to try to show one very powerful Arab just how the trick might be done.

It was John Connally's turn to take a hand. Connally had a good friend named Sheik Khaled ben Mafouz. Mafouz, an immensely wealthy man, was the chief operating officer of the National Commercial Bank of Jidda, which his family controlled. In February 1978, Mafouz took over an entire floor of the Mayflower Hotel in Washington and installed himself there with his forty bodyguards. Among his visitors were John Connally and Nelson Bunker Hunt. Mafouz, like the shah, made no move, but Bunker was getting himself widely known around the Gulf as a man who saw great possibilities in silver.

He was also active on his own behalf. Bunker kept a number of his Thoroughbreds at a French stable in Chantilly managed by Maurice Zilber, an Egyptian-born Jew. By a happy chance, another of Zilber's customers was a naturalized Saudi of Lebanese extraction named Mahmoud Fustock. Fustock's sister, Aida, was once married to Prince Abdullah, the commander of the Saudi National Guard and third in line for the throne, and Fustock himself enjoyed the prince's confidence. He was in fact, a wakeel—roughly the equivalent of a nineteenth-century British nobleman's man of business. Fronting for his prince, the wakeel makes investments, channels the profits into the treasury and the privy purse, and assumes any losses in his own name. There exists no reliable estimate of Fustock's personal wealth, in part because it is difficult to tell when he is investing in his own right and when he is acting on behalf of Abdullah and, it is said, Abdullah's son, Prince Faisal.

Around the beginning of 1979, Fustock began to be seen in the company of Naji Robert Nahas, whose name means "copper" in Arabic. Nahas also raced horses and knew Zilber, the stable owner—and had likewise made Bunker's acquaintance; on July 25, in Kentucky, advised by Zilber, he bought eleven of Bunker's yearlings for $1.1 million. He was receptive to the idea of a commodities play, having already made a fortune in coffee futures, and he was in contact with Norton Waltuch, a trader and vice president of Continental Grain's trading subsidiary, Conti Commodities. Shortly after Waltuch successfully cornered the orange juice market following the Florida freeze of 1977, he was contacted by Nahas, who expressed an interest in joining the play. It was too late, and Waltuch suggested silver instead. Nahas proved agreeable. On at least one occasion when Waltuch met Bunker in Paris to discuss silver, Nahas was present. In May, Waltuch also met with Fustock. Nahas was there. Bunker, Nahas, and Fustock formed a syndicate.

To avoid damaging leaks, the number of principals had to be kept small; and to foil possible countermoves by rivals, the exchanges, and government agencies, the operation had to be made as confusing as possible. Nahas established a silver trading account with Waltuch at Conti. The syndicate brought in the Geneva investment firm of Advicorp, headed by Jean-Jacques Bally and Pierre-Alain Hirshey, who established personal accounts at Conti and at another commodities broker, ACLI International. Robert Ramsey, Nahas' associate, established an account at Conti. Fustock established an account at Merrill Lynch, where Herbert Hunt did much of his trading. Other monies were handled anonymously by Banque Populaire, which established accounts at ACLI and Conti, and by

Gillian Financial of Geneva, which traded at Conti. Conti took other money and subdivided it, for bookkeeping purposes, between ContiCapital Management and ContiCapital Ltd. of Nassau in the Bahamas. The syndicate set up a shell corporation in Panama—Litardex—with Nahas as president and a vice president from Advicorp; Advicorp controlled its account. Advi also controlled the Banque Populaire, Gillian, and Fustock accounts. Nahas controlled others—between them, Nahas and Advicorp controlled ten foreign silver accounts at ACLI alone. Bunker and Herbert set up a Bermuda venture, International Metals Investment Company, Ltd. (IMIC), in partnership with Sheik Mohammad Aboud al-Amoudi and Sheik Ali bin Mussalem, relatively small fry by Saudi standards but associated with Abdullah's son, Faisal. The syndicate had established a trading position and they had achieved maximum confusion. They were almost ready to go.

There was one other thing to do. The U.S. government's silver stockpile had to be immobilized.

The 139-million-ounce stockpile was under the control of the General Services Administration, and the GSA was none too happy about it. The government no longer mints silver coins, and the stuff just sits there, taking up space. The government had sold silver regularly until 1970. Now it was trying to sell some of it again. If it did, the Hunts and their syndicate were going to buy it—otherwise, it could be the Banco de Mexico all over again, with a major influx eating dangerously into their capital. The initial government sale, proposed in 1978, was to be of 62.5 million ounces, a figure later reduced to 15 million ounces when fears were voiced that such a large amount of silver would disrupt the market. Fifteen million ounces was better, but it still wasn't good. It would have to be bought up, it would put the government back in the market, and one sale has a way of leading to another.

Over the objections of those reliable Hunt allies Jesse Helms and Strom Thurmond, the sale was approved by the

Senate in October 1978, but the House failed to act until June 28, 1979, when Congressman Larry McDonald introduced a bill that would require the government to buy—not sell—$513 million worth of silver. The cosponsors were Steve Symms of Idaho and Richard Kelly of Florida. It was, by most standards, a frivolous piece of legislation, but it stopped the projected sale cold. The Hunts had nothing to fear from that quarter.

Between the end of 1978 and March 1979, the Hunts increased the number of their silver contracts from 5,393 to 8,354, and the price of silver began to move up. Exchange officials later made much of the fact that the movement was spontaneous, a result of the reliable old law of supply and demand rather than the machinations of the Hunts, but the exchange officials have a vested interest in proving that the Hunts never did anything. Their trading floors are among the last strongholds of unfettered free enterprise on earth, and their private nightmare is government regulation. They have therefore chosen to ignore that the price-escalating silver shortage was in some part caused by the enormous amount of silver the Hunts had already withdrawn from trading: the Zurich horde, the silver they owned in the vaults of CBOT and COMEX—and the 41,770,000 ounces they had tied up in contracts. In all, they controlled perhaps 120 million ounces, and if they did not yet control the market itself, they could make it move. Silver rose to almost $9 an ounce in July 1979. This time, there was to be no sudden rush into the market. This time, they weren't coming down like the wolf on the fold. This time, they were going to do it right.

By the end of August, with the threat of a market overhang from the government stockpile eliminated by McDonald, Symms, and Kelly, the syndicate was ready.

At the end of that month, as the price reached $10.15 an ounce, the CFTC made an astonishing and puzzling discovery. Five accounts, handled by Waltuch and traded on COMEX, had established net long positions aggregating 8,560 contracts, or 42,800,000 ounces. These accounts were owned by Nahas, Banque Populaire, Gillian ContiCapital Management, ContiCapital Ltd., and Waltuch himself, and they were concentrated in the December contract. Furthermore, the Hunts' Bermuda-based International Metals Investment Company had established a CBOT and COMEX position of another 42 million ounces. The CFTC had no idea who IMIC represented. The commission appears to have been unaware of the Fustock, Ramsey, and Litardex accounts, and it paid little attention to other positions at Bache, ACLI, and Merrill Lynch, possibly because Waltuch seemed to go out of his way to call attention to himself. It became his practice to stride conspicuously across the floor in his orange Conti jacket, the world's greatest silver long. As he approached the pit, everybody but the futures commodities merchants representing the commercial users and sellers got out. He bid up limit.

Everybody knew a squeeze was on, but nobody could prove it. Everybody knew that Norton Waltuch commanded the vanguard, but nobody could prove that either. That there was a guiding intelligence was clear, and its identity was suspected, but it, too, was impervious to proof. The head of the exchange tried to order Waltuch off the floor and failed. The CFTC dithered.

Another odd thing happened. Norton Waltuch bought no more silver for his own account after August. (Later, in December, trading against his own clients and the Hunts, he began to liquidate his position. In the process, he made between $10 and $20 million while everybody else was taking a bath.)

With the CFTC seemingly transfixed by a hooded figure gesturing hypnotically in the middle distance, the exchanges took steps. They knew a cornering operation was going on and that the Hunts had all but destroyed speculation. So the exchanges' boards of directors began to experiment with ways of bringing the madness to a halt. The daily market limits were widened and initial margin was increased—from $1,000 to $1,750 at CBOT and from $1,500 to $5,000 at COMEX. It was too late. With the bulk of the speculators driven out of the market and the price of silver escalating, the Hunts had the first stage of their pyramid: they were cleaning up on variation margin. It was time to drive the price higher still by removing some more silver from circulation.

In September, the Hunts' IMIC took delivery of 5,920,000 ounces, Banque Populaire took 4,575,000 ounces, and Nahas took 2,750,000 ounces. In October, IMIC took an additional 6,720,000 ounces and Banque Populaire took another 3,960,000 ounces. Silver hit $17 an ounce. IMIC further strengthened its reserves by arranging EFPs (exchanges of futures for physical) totaling 27 million ounces with the bullion houses of Mocatta in New York and Sharps Pixley in London. Whether, as the Hunts later claimed, the deal saved Mocatta and Dr. Jarecki from serious financial embarrassment cannot be determined; everybody tells a different story. Since they involved bullion, coins, and forward contracts, the two EFPs had no immediate effect on the market, but they further reduced the world's supply.

In late September, COMEX increased margin to a staggering $50,000 per contract in the spot month, and CBOT increased their initial margin to $4,000 (a fourfold increase in less than a month). On October 3, CBOT further increased margin to $30,000 per contract on all existing and future positions of 300 or more contracts. The CFTC finally found out who owned IMIC and asked Bunker to stop by the office for a chat. With a brazenness that is almost admirable, he told the commissioners that he knew no Arabs other than his two partners and that he hadn't even met al-Amoudi. He also announced that he was exchanging silver in American vaults for silver in London and Zurich. He said he was doing so because he was afraid the government might try to take it away from him, the way it had taken away gold in 1932. The CFTC placed a report of the conversation in its files and did nothing.

Meanwhile, something had gone wrong, although nobody

noticed it at the time. Minpeco, the Peruvian government's silver-marketing agency, took short contracts for 13.5 million ounces in October. A short position is a gamble that the market will decline, and the gamble looked reasonable. The CFTC, still officially unaware of what was happening, learned that Comex had managed to negotiate a confidential agreement whereby Nahas, Banque Populaire, and Waltuch would reduce their position in the December contract, thus reducing the pressure on the shorts. On October 19, the COMEX price stood at $17.46 an ounce. By October 26, the day the supposedly secret agreement took effect, the price had dropped to $16.35, and the Peruvians seemed justified in their gamble. However, on the day before, October 25, David Rockefeller and Henry Kissinger finally prevailed over the objections of the State Department, and the shah of Iran was admitted to the country for medical treatment. On November 4, the American embassy in Teheran was seized. In times of crisis, as mentioned earlier, money runs to precious metals. The price of silver began to go up again. By November 30, it was $18.76 an ounce, and the Peruvians were faced with a dilemma. Either they were going to have to come up with 13.5 million ounces of silver, which they didn't have, or they were going to have to assume an offsetting long position, take an $80 million loss, and run the market up further. The decision had to be made soon.

Unaware of the Peruvians' mounting problem, Bunker and Herbert were sitting pretty. At the end of October, the Hunts and IMIC owned 26 percent of the silver in the COMEX vaults and 62 percent of CBOT's. As a result of the Mocatta and Sharps Pixley EFP transactions, IMIC owned an additional 27 million ounces that were outside the market altogether, and the transfer of ownership to London and Zurich was proceeding smoothly. If they were following the same plan that Boswell was pursuing, it was now time to achieve a position of influence in a brokerage house, and that is exactly what they did. Capitalizing on the takeover fears of Harry A.

Jacobs, Jr., the chairman of Bache, the brothers bought 6.5 percent of the firm's stock, each taking a half participation to evade the SEC's disclosure rules. It was an ideal transaction. The Hunts were already doing a gigantic business with the firm, which gave them the considerable advantages enjoyed by very favored customers. Now they were major stock-holders and objects of the chairman's gratitude. Unusual influence over disposition of the firm's assets were ensured.

Things were looking good. Until the Iranian crisis drove scared money into metal, Waltuch's antics and the new high margins kept speculation to a minimum—a desirable thing. It was time to complete the pyramid.

With the exception of the contracts purchased at the beginning of the year and a few other contracts adjusted for tax purposes, the bulk of the Hunts' position consisted of silver bought at around $9 an ounce. With the warehouse receipts from this silver as collateral, they raised $267,836,600 from brokerage houses and Swiss and American banks by August 1, 1979. With silver now trading at more than four times $4, it was possible to take the very same warehouse receipts and go to the well again, obtaining the money to squeeze the shorts out of existence, scoop up all but a small remnant of the exchange silver (leaving enough in other hands to keep the market functioning but under their control), and move on to the final phase of the operation—the issuance of silver-indexed negotiable bonds that would give them their own hard currency and allow them to have their cake and eat it too.

They borrowed an additional $136,290,800—$66,290,800 from ACLI, $37 million from Bache, $15 million from Credit Lyonnais, $8 million from the J. Henry Schroder Bank & Trust Co., and $10 million from First National Bank of Chicago. IMIC, moving into debt for the first time, borrowed $50 million from Merrill Lynch, $10 million from the Schroder Bank of Zurich, $25 million from Citibank, $150 million from the Swiss Bank Corporation, $25,482,060 from Mocatta, and $12,003,000 from various other U.S. banks. By the end of the year, the brothers and IMIC had $408,775,860 in new funds. It is not known how much the other members of the syndicate raised. But it should have been enough. It wasn't.

November was quiet; CBOT reduced its margins. Silver reached $18.81 on November 30. On December 14, it hit $21.65 and it stood at $29.35 on December 28. The Hunts didn't seem to realize it, but they had just lost control of the market. The Peruvians took their medicine: they assumed an offsetting position and went long 13.5 million ounces, driving the market up further. With Islam distracted by Mr. Rockefeller's crisis, the Russians invaded Afghanistan, and more money began to pour in. CBOT raised its margins again, but it did no good. Silver was off on a ride that wouldn't end until March 28, and the Hunts were as good as dead.

At first it didn't look too bad; in fact, it looked wonderful. The syndicate had plenty of money. On December 27, it controlled 53 percent of the COMEX stocks and 69 percent of CBOT's, up from 26 to 62 percent in October. The abrupt jump in price meant that money, a lot of it, came flowing in from the shorts. Unfortunately, the syndicate also held 57 percent of the outstanding obligations in the March contract, and by March the market would be completely out of whack.

On January 4, silver reached $36.10, and the exchanges again tried to strike back. COMEX established position limits of 500 contracts in January and February and 2,000 contracts in all other months, meaning that nobody could buy more than the stated number. Bunker and Herbert were later to make much of this and other restrictive actions, pointing to the large number of shorts among the membership of the CBOT and COMEX boards of directors and claiming that they unfairly changed the rules in the middle of the game. Here is irony. The exchanges are near perfect examples of the sort of free-enterprise capitalism Bunker has long extolled, and he should have been aware that they had a perfect right to change the rules anytime they felt like it; the Hunts themselves are notorious hardball players, and beating up on business opponents is their favorite recreation.

Meanwhile, the CFTC, the important agent of that creeping socialism Bunker so deplores, did absolutely nothing; if it had possessed the power or the will to act, it might actually have helped him out by stabilizing the market. Furthermore, although the rule changes made the game more costly and difficult, they weren't the Hunts' main problem. It was the Banco de Mexico all over again, it was the sugar play all over again. The price was skyrocketing and the syndicate was getting hit with new silver from all directions. People melted down their flatware and their tea sets, perhaps as much as 36 million ounces of them. Coin hoards suddenly appeared, and volumes of Indian silver flowed in through the smugglers' market in Dubai. Formerly unprofitable mine shafts were reopened, and the refiners increased their output. The CFTC estimates that as much as 90 million new ounces appeared in this manner, and the figure was probably higher; COMEX and CBOT silver stocks began to rise again. If the syndicate was to retain its edge, it was going to have to buy up that silver too, and the new rules made it hard. Bunker established new accounts, one of them in the name of his horse trainer, and Nahas followed suit, but there was too much coming in for them to handle and it was coming in too fast. The market was reacting on its own again, and a downward break was only a matter of time.

The Hunts almost immediately made matters worse for themselves. Still moving the silver out of the country in mid-January, they engaged in a number of EFPs that threw the London price out of line with the New York price, creating a backwardation that drove the price up further as the FCMs arbitraged the spread, playing the two markets off against each other. On January 21, COMEX limited trading to liquidation only and CBOT followed suit the next day. On February 4, with silver finally stable at around $35, COMEX increased margins again, to $60,000 on positions of 251 or more contracts, and made them retroactive, cutting further into the syndicate's capital.

Capital was once more beginning to be a problem. The Hunts took large deliveries in early February and rolled the bulk of their contracts forward into months unaffected by the emergency rules, but their position was no longer good. They still owned a lot of $4 silver, but it wasn't $4 silver anymore. In the language of the market, it was priced to spot on the day they rolled it, and the vault silver was mortgaged at the rate prevailing when the loan was taken. February silver was drifting between $32 and $37, and they were getting some margin and collateral calls. The 90 million or more ounces of new silver had taken the pressure off the shorts, the rise in price had reduced its value as an inflationary hedge, and there were signs that crisis buying was slacking off in all precious metals. The syndicate was in danger of finding itself alone on the long side of the market, with a lot of gleeful shorts on the other side. Unless they could come up with some more money and come up with it soon, they would not only fail in their great goal, but they would be faced with a falling market.

In early March, Bunker went out to the Gulf again. Exactly what he did there is a little vague, but he seems to have tried to raise some more money from the Gulf Investment Company, a consortium of Kuwaitis and Bahrainis who had previously traded very successfully through Bank BAII, netting around $22 million when they bailed out of the market in January. They had been eager to try their luck again, and they joined with the Hunts in a new company called Gulf Precious Metals, capitalized at $500 million, of which the Hunts were to put up between 10 and 20 percent. Whether because they sensed the weakness of the market or for some other reason, the Arabs had neglected to produce their share, and Bunker had come to persuade them. He failed. There wasn't going to be any more money unless the Hunts and their partners raised it themselves.

On March 14, the New York market fell to $21 an ounce. To call it a market anymore was a misnomer: it was a shearing operation, and the Hunts and their syndicate were the sheep. They were trapped. They couldn't have gone short even if they'd wanted to. In the pure, untrammeled capitalistic system the Hunts and their friends had gotten mixed up in, there had to be a buyer for every seller, a seller for every buyer, and they were virtually alone on the long side of the market. It was a ridiculous situation. They owned most of the available silver in the world, and they needed some more paper money. Collateral calls from the banks were eating into their stockpile and margin calls were eating into their cash. The brothers began mortgaging their oil leases. They took loans from the family's privately owned oil company. They took loans from ACLI and Bache and Merrill Lynch and E. F. Hutton. They drew down new lines of bank credit. Nahas put up his ships. The free enterprise system ground on and on. The Hunts' margin calls were running in the vicinity of $10 million a day.

It couldn't continue. Not only were the brothers running through their own money, but they were placing portions of the family fortune in jeopardy. As great fortunes go, the Hunt patrimony is set up in a rather peculiar manner. In fact, it is set up exactly as one might expect from a small-time cardsharp of preternatural shrewdness, such as H. L. Hunt. Because he placed the bulk of his fortune in trust for his children in 1935, just before the New Dealers changed the law, he was able to pass on the money virtually unencumbered by taxes. Unlike other plutocrats of the period, however, he did not place the trusts in the care of a bank. Instead, he placed them in the hands of his cronies and lawyers—people he could control, and through whom he could continue to control his wealth. He likewise vested his children with complete legal ownership of the crown jewels of his empire, Placid Oil and Penrod Drilling, which similarly enabled him to remain in command. As the children—Margaret, Catherine, Bunker,

Herbert, and Lamar; all of them but the mentally ill Hassie—reached maturity, they replaced their father's men on the boards of each other's trusts and assumed leadership of their companies. With the presiding genius of their father now absent from the scene, they devised a cabinet system whereby they met regularly to devise investment and business strategies, with Bunker and Herbert more or less presiding as firsts among equals.

It all seems very unsophisticated, especially compared to the Rockefeller family offices, but in practice it worked wonderfully. The cabinet system and the interlocking trusts meant that the fortune continued to function as a single unit, just as it had in the old man's day; the Hunt siblings, rather than the trust officers of some bank, dictated what happened to the money. And because Penrod and Placid—now grown to be the largest privately owned oil company in the world—possessed no stockholders outside the family, the Hunts could move with great secrecy and speed; in effect, they reported to no one but the IRS. Great Western United, as a public company subject to many disclosure rules, was an aberration, but after the failure of the Sunshine initiative the brothers bought out the surviving stockholders and made it private, too. It was an old-fashioned way of doing things, but it made them richer than the Rockefellers.

The danger in the system was that one or more of the siblings might lead the entire family into jeopardy, as Bunker and Herbert had just done. The silver play no longer looked like the amassing of an invincible store of value; it looked like pouring money down a rathole, and now Placid and the Louisiana oil fields were being drawn in. Perhaps their strong-willed sister Margaret finally put her foot down, perhaps the brothers just decided that their string had run out, but a decision was reached. The Hunts decided to place the world's financial system in peril rather than lose any more money.

On March 25, Herbert informed Bache that they couldn't make a $135 million margin call. It was another gamble. Either the market would rescue itself or it wouldn't, but at some point the federal government was going to have to intervene, either to save the situation or to forestall a second crash when the syndicate's enormous silver supply threatened to go into liquidation. It might work or it might not—many things could go wrong—but the government was their best hope now. That was the reality of the situation. Whether the Hunts quite grasped it is an open question, and not even Bunker's subsequent peculiar behavior quite answers it.

He and his brother no longer controlled the market—the shorts did—but he could still make it crash, and that is exactly what he did. Their debt was enormous. They owed ACLI $134,258,000, Bache $233,430,300, E. F. Hutton $100 million, and Merrill Lynch $102,501,200. Their bank debt had grown to $359 million. They owed Placid $105 million. Herbert owed Bunker $40,500,000. IMIC owed Merrill Lynch $287,750,000, Mocatta $17,677,000, and various banks $161 million. There was an upcoming forward contract with Engelhard Minerals of $665 million—19 million ounces at the old $35 an ounce price—and they were locked into it. The brokerages began to sell off the warehouse receipts they held as collateral. The banks held more receipts. The brothers were in danger of losing it all—not the family fortune, although the catastrophe would have taken a healthy bite out of it, but the silver itself. There was only one ray of hope. The CFTC had finally begun to meet with the Treasury and the Federal Reserve, and Chairman Paul Volcker himself was involved. The government was still doing nothing, but its attention had been attracted at last. Something might be done.

It is impossible to know the state of Bunker's mind on March 26, but what he did is clear enough. At 8 P.M. Paris time (2 P.M. in New York), he announced that he, Fustock, Nahas, al-Amoudi, and Prince Faisal were prepared to issue silver-backed bonds. Maybe it was nothing but a last-ditch play to raise some money, a premature implementation of a long-maturing plan, a last desperate plunge. On the other hand, perhaps it was a coolly calculated risk. The Hunts may have never known much about business, but they all know how to gamble.

Bunker's announcement broke the back of the market, such as it was. If the traders needed a signal that the Hunts were finally, completely, out of money, they could not have received a clearer one. The price of silver dropped $5, to $10.89 an ounce, and panic began to spread beyond the silver pit. Then it began to spread beyond the exchange. Things began to look very bad indeed; Silver Thursday, March 27, 1980, began to bear a disquieting resemblance to a certain Thursday in October, just over fifty years before.

Whether Bunker intended it that way or not, the gamble paid off. The exchanges, fearing that they would never reopen, refused to close. On Friday, March 28, Bache and the other brokerages continued to unload Hunt silver, and it seemed inevitable that the price would continue to spiral downward. But it didn't. Instead, somebody—a syndicate put together in secret by Dr. Jarecki, it is said—bought a billion dollars' worth of silver at bargain-basement prices, and by the end of the day, the price had stabilized at $12 an ounce. It would remain stable. More, it would rise modestly, rewarding the Jarecki syndicate (or whoever) with a handsome profit. Thanks to its sales of the Hunt collateral, Bache did not go under; it reported the most profitable year in its history.

The Hunts didn't have to pay Engelhard the $665 million, nor did they have to part with the silver they had left after the margin calls were satisfied—the bullion in Zurich is safe for the moment, its precise or even approximate quantity unknown, and during the subsequent congressional testimony, neither Bunker nor Herbert mentioned Zurich at all. With the Federal Reserve standing as a keenly interested spectator in the wings, the Hunts were able to form themselves into a general partnership with Placid (which is more than a little like forming a general partnership with your foot), putting up their coal, their gold, their racehorses, and their oil leases in the Beaufort Sea. In return they obtained $1.1 billion in new bank money to repay their debts. It is roughly the same amount that the Chrysler Corporation was able to obtain with considerably more hullaballoo. Congressman Kelly, who was fierce in his opposition to the Chrysler guarantee, was strangely silent on the subject of the Hunts' silver despite the Fed's involvement. And although the interest payments were staggering, the world was spared the spectacle of the Hunt brothers walking the streets without a pair of silver dimes to rub together.

True, poor Nahas lost his ships and between $2 and $3 million in cash, and his trading losses cost Conti around $10 million after the tax write-off, but Norton Waltuch made at least that much and probably more. True, too, the Saudis were not too pleased with their adventure and are unlikely to trust the Hunts or dabble in silver in the foreseeable future— Abdullah may have lost in the vicinity of $1 billion—and this may actually be a good thing. (al-Amoudi was apparently compensated for his personal losses with new construction contracts in his native land, where the pie is large.) A few silverware manufacturers had some rocky months, the price of photographic paper, X-ray film, and hearing-aid batteries rose, and a few small investors followed the Hunts and lost their shirts. All in all, the whole caper appears to be another romance of capitalism, where the unwise have been punished (but not too severely) and the invisible hand has again worked its magic to save the day with minimal loss. Why, then, should anyone be concerned?

The trouble is that nothing happens in isolation. Between them, the Hunt brothers and David Rockefeller very nearly succeeded in disrupting the world's financial order, although the Hunt brothers and David Rockefeller were each trying to do something very different. Rockefeller was trying to save his bank from an $800 million loss whose effects would have been particularly aggravating in the light of the fact that the bank was recovering from the crisis of 1974–76. The crisis of 1974–76, in turn, was a direct result of loans to such stricken giants of the forest as Penn Central and W. T. Grant, combined with such sins of liability management as Fed Funds, negotiable CDs, and commercial paper, and it was liability management that enabled many of those loans to be made in the first place, often in defiance of the monetary policies of the Treasury and the Fed.

Nor must we forget the disastrous mismanagement of REITS. Crisis at home combined with a major new influx of funds from OPEC to encourage the major banks to export as much of their business as possible to the Euromarket, where the profits were. But many of these profits resulted from rolling the debt of the richer less-developed countries, which placed the banks in the Alice-in-Wonderland situation of claiming profits based on the money they had lent. The unrestrained lending in the Euromarket—where, incidentally, Mr. Rockefeller's Iranians had elected to park the bulk of their deposits—in turn generated a certain uncontrollable amount of inflation through the operation of the multiplier effect. This inflation, in turn, combined with the antics of Colonel Qaddafi and the family's apocalyptic politics to encourage the Hunt brothers to seek a store of value that was impervious to outside threats. Which meant that they had to take over the world's silver supply. Which meant in turn—in nicely circular fashion—that they needed to recruit from those very Gulf potentates whose deposits were causing the mischief to begin with. One has to admit that it all has a rather tidy symmetry to it.

Then there is the small matter of the Hunts' $1.1 billion loan, given with the Fed's blessing to pay off debts incurred in defiance of the Fed's own loudly expressed strictures about speculative borrowing. There are wheels within wheels here, but the important things to remember are that the original debt came from somewhere; that the banks and the brokerage houses made the loans to fund a takeover of the world's silver supply; and that by applying its influence to the making of the consolidated loan, the Fed again betrayed a disquieting tendency to ratify a danger rather than abolish it. Nor did the Fed betray much of an inclination to enforce its own rules; despite the energetic prodding of Congressman Benjamin Rosenthal, the Fed did nothing to force the Hunts to divest themselves of the silver, which was the principal condition underlying the loan. It appears that the Hunts have gotten away scot-free once again.

Finally, there is the matter of money itself. Bunker was perfectly right about money, of course. Since it severed the currency from gold a decade ago, the government has indeed been in the wallpaper business, just as Bunker insists, with its folding money backed by nothing but faith and magic. There is even a futures market in various forms of specie now, as though it were a crop whose value has to be determined by speculation.

Here one sees the peculiar beauty of the brothers' hard-currency scheme. Simply put, silver-backed currency (had it been printed) would have solved a big problem of modern business. Assume you are a large company. Assume you need to purchase some generators. Generators are enormous and costly objects, and they are made to order. This takes time. Time, in a world where money fluctuates, is no longer the businessman's friend. In agreeing on the price of the generators, both the buyer and the seller must make a gambler's guess concerning the value of money at the time of delivery. The one who guesses wrong loses—unless, of course, he has constructed a prudent and effective hedge in the international money market, a gamble in itself. Bunker bucks, as they might have been known, would have been an elegant solution to the dilemma. With the Hunts and their syndicate in control of silver, the value of Bunker bucks would not have fluctuated. As the world's only stable currency, they would have been much in demand.

No one knows what would have happened if the Hunts

had succeeded, whether to use silver as a bartering medium or to print their own hard currency or whatever else might have occurred to their fertile, if erratic, imaginations. Certainly they would have become a power in the West, a power of incalculable magnitude, entirely private, politically strange, and curiously ignorant or contemptuous of the problems of mortals less rich. The Hunts have presented us with an old problem, but in a new way. It concerns malefactors of great wealth.

For the first time since the days of the robber barons, we are witnessing a vast new concentration of wealth in a relatively few hands. It is an unknown factor, this concentration of the world's treasure, and its implications are various, unpleasant, and vague; but the Hunts demonstrated at least one application to which it might be put. They failed, and they are unlikely to find the Saudi purses open to them again. But they have established a precedent, and other men have fertile imaginations, too. Presently, within a decade or less, the Saudi development program will come to an end, and their cash accumulation is likely to advance from the remarkable to the fabulous. Doubtless they will want to put it to some good use. Indeed, they will have to put it to use or run the risk of standing in the same relation to the United States that the United States stood to India in the 1960s: they will end up owning a dangerously big piece of a currency based on faith and magic. It is a situation rich with possibilities. The Hunts suggested one. Doubtless other men, equally inventive and plausible, will suggest others. Perhaps next time, they will succeed.

6.

What Is To Be Done?

The decade began with the largest business failure in
American history. It ended with the Hunt brothers' silver
play. Between these bracketing events, the world changed,
and it is unlikely that it will ever be the same again. From the
grim perspective of the eighties, the collapse of the Penn Central seems almost comfortingly traditional. A company got itself into a pack of trouble, ran out of money, and went
bankrupt. Nothing too terribly unusual there, except perhaps
the colossal ineptitude when the merger was attempted,
David Bevan's trail-blazing use of commercial paper as a substitute for long-term financing, and his dipping into the Euromarket for emergency funds. If the fiasco taught any lesson
beyond the obvious ones—i.e., if you are going to run a giant
enterprise, it is wise to know what you're doing, and it is seldom a good idea to have a management team whose members
detest each other—it is this: great banks, in their eagerness to
drum up some business, are perhaps not as careful as their
depositors have a right to expect. Indeed, as the decade pro-
gressed, carelessness became a kind of watchword in those
halls of private finance where, as we have seen, so much of
the country's economic policy is formulated and implemented

by men whose first allegiance is to the appearance of their balance sheets rather than to the public weal or to reality.

Even as, on the domestic scene, the banks learned how to manufacture their own currency and thwart the policy of the Federal Reserve (constructing, in the process, an unprecedented concentration of debt), a single great fact began to emerge in the form of the OPEC deposits in the Euromarket. These deposits, in turn, offered both a simple opportunity for the banks to redeem what had been lost in the mismanaged domestic economy, to which mismanagement their own contribution was not small; and posed the sort of threat that is inevitably posed by vast sums of money arriving all at once, and controlled by people whose interests do not necessarily coincide with those of the banks or of the world economic order. The OPEC deposits not only enabled American banks to further circumvent the monetary policies of the federal government, but they also assisted the great multinational banks to weather the mid-decade crisis and the REIT fiasco. In varying degrees, these institutions had become progressively less American; freed from governmental restraints by the magic of the Euromarket, they had become international adventurers, knowing no master but themselves.

The price of oil has doubled four times since 1970. As I write these words in a burning borough of a capital-starved city where a long night of barbarism seems to be settling over the poorest inhabitants, Brazil has become the greatest bank debtor in the history of the world. The country owes in the vicinity of $60 billion, half (and perhaps more than half) of it to U.S. banks, with the bulk of it concentrated in the Euromarket. It is an old saw in the trade that an imposing debtor owns the bank from which he borrows, because the bank can no longer afford to allow him to go broke. In a way, then, Brazil's monstrous debt is somewhat like the equally monstrous debt of the American industrial establishment; since the banks have persisted in covering it in the vain expectation of a miracle due any Tuesday, they have allowed it to swell to the point where they are obliged to refund and add to it, and the devil take the law of diminishing returns. A game like that has only one ending, and the wonder is that we haven't arrived there before now. Meanwhile, the OPEC deposits have become so vital to the process that at least one international banker, David Rockefeller, has given powerful indications that he will do anything, go to any length, to avoid losing a major portion of them. And liability financing has combined with the multiplier effect to create an inflation that worked powerfully on the creative mind of Nelson Bunker Hunt, and for the third time in a decade the entire house of cards was in danger of crashing down.

So, as Lenin once asked in circumstances that are perhaps a trifle more similar to the present dilemma than one would like to admit: What is to be done? It is far easier to describe what has already been done, which is nothing. The situation remains very fragile. The Brazilians have made valiant efforts to develop technologies that would enable their cars and industries to run on food, but their progress has been token at best. The clock is still running in Brazil, and the mathematics of the situation point to default—although, if it comes, the bankers will take care to call it something else, such as "rescheduling." Buzz words aside, the fact remains that no one in the world knows what might happen if the Brazilians' $60 billion suddenly went bad, since no country in the history of the world has ever amassed such a debt. Perhaps our luck will hold. Perhaps the Brazilians will stumble on an oil pool or discover a method of distilling fuel out of mud and dandelions; perhaps the Northern Hemisphere will vaporize in a transpolar exchange of nuclear missiles or fall prey to a meteor shower, rendering the whole question moot. The reality of the situation is simple: either the Brazilians are going to pay back the money or they aren't, and the banking system of the West can't keep making narrow escapes forever.

Meanwhile, the Saudis are on the verge of taking ownership of a large hunk of the national currency, adding the leverage of money to the very considerable leverage of oil they already hold. And there is more. As the Saudi penetration into the currency rises, the export dividend will dwindle, and for the same reason: the effective end of the boom days in Saudi domestic development, upsetting the rough balance that presently exists in the terms of trade. We are viewing a strange kind of seamless whole here, with a potential Brazilian default and vastly increased Saudi leverage serving as interwoven threads of the same grim tapestry. The political dangers are well known, the economic consequences hardly discussed; yet it can hardly strike the reflective mind as a terrific idea to have the fate of the world's financial system locked in symbiosis with a dictatorship in an ongoing solvency crisis (a crisis caused by oil) and a feudal kingdom with a minuscule population that is rapidly approaching the saturation point for goods and services. And even this is what one might call a best-case analysis that ignores the political ramifications and assumes the stability of a pair of regimes in regions that have no history of stability at all.

Are the vast reservoirs of petroleum surrounding the Gulf, then, to be our subterranean seas of destiny? In the short run, it would seem so. Once it was steel and coal and trade that drove the engines of finance; now it is dollars and oil and the whims and lifespans of princes—whether they will keep their thrones, whether they will decide to purchase the world's vanadium, the way the royal cat will jump, provided it lives. It is not merely a fragile situation that grows more brittle with each passing hour; it is also a rather nasty one, but we will tamper with it at our peril. We have seen too much tampering already, with consequences that have been unforeseen, and most of the recommended remedies happen to be surreal in their irrelevance.

The banker's solution is perhaps the simplest: ease the regulations to make the domestic banking function like the Euromarket, thus attracting limitless amounts of capital to our shores. Every fox wants to sign on as a security guard at the chicken coop, and bankers are no exception. How they will cope with a further acceleration in the velocity of money and the operation of the multiplier effect they do not say, but the profits would certainly be very nice, at least for a while.

Or we might return to the gold standard. It has its undeniable attractions. A return to gold would pretty much put paid to currency fluctuations, since the government would establish the price of the metal (as it did until 1966), and maintain it much as the Hunts proposed to maintain the price of silver. As a way of forcing a country to live within its means (as defined by the amount of gold it owns) the gold standard is close to unbeatable, or so the argument goes, since the only way to inflate the currency is to repeal the legislation that established the standard to begin with. The fans of gold live in a very happy world, where inflation is a thing of the past and the businessman can sail his corporate sea with a measure of serenity. Another word for it is a fool's paradise.

The full benefits of a gold standard are only realized when a nation is in control of its currency, including all privately issued negotiable instruments. But the country is not in control of its currency. Negotiable CDs, letters of credit, and even personal checks (when they are traded from hand to hand before returning to their bank of origin—the technical term is "playing the float") amount to a private issue of currency that distorts national monetary policy. With the public currency rendered finite and expensive by the gold standard, private currency can be expected to flourish as the bankers and the businessmen seek to keep the marketplace as liquid as possible, bringing Gresham's Law into operation. Cheap money is more attractive than expensive money.

Privately issued negotiable instruments are cheaper than gold-based official money, if only because they are theoretically infinite, whereas gold-based official money is rigidly finite, and in times of general economic expansion, one is forced to pay a premium to obtain it. Private instruments are under no such constraints; their issue is limited only by the

well-known prudence of the bankers, who invented them to
evade far more flexible controls than would exist under gold.
We therefore end up with a classical example of a dual currency system, with the cheaper, more attractive currency coming under the control of the most powerful corporations and
their bankers—an obviously unhealthy situation. As Gresham
foresaw, the cheaper money begins to drive out the expensive
money by dint of its popularity and fluidity, but Gresham
lived in simpler times and a modification is required. Privately
issued cheap money amounts, as always, to an inflation of the
currency, but the private instruments are denominated in
gold-based dollars and, like any such instrument, they are
eventually cashed. And since gold has rendered the official
currency finite, every time a private instrument is cashed, it
effects a draw-down of the money supply available to citizens
lacking access to such corporate currencies of preference,
amounting to an unplanned deflation. The official money is
made even more expensive, the private currency is made even
more attractive, especially during flush times for the corporations, when many private instruments circulate—and the government can make up the deficit only with fresh purchases of
gold. Either that, or it can allow consumer credit to disappear, with consequences that are unpredictable. Nothing has
been solved by gold: control of the money supply has been
lost, not gained, and the government's options are limited to a
choice between buying more gold or accepting a consumer
recession—in other words, we are back to where we started,
but a little worse off.

    With the money supply limited by the gold supply, the
Fed can no longer attempt to work its countercyclical Keyne-
sian magic, tightening money in booms and releasing more of
the stuff in slumps; that decision is now in private hands and
is no longer a matter of policy. While such an eventuality will
doubtless bring glad cries of rejoicing from conservatives, it
ought to be borne in mind that the last time gold ruled the
economy, hair-raising depressions were the order of the day,

and the existence of private currencies adds an incalculable new dimension. But it gets worse.

At the time of the Penn Central collapse and the subsequent runoff of commercial paper, the Federal Reserve saved the day with its discount window. The steady flow of loans from the bottomless federal pocket quickly quelled the panic, but the story might be dramatically different under the gold standard and its finite currency. All flexibility is lost; the government's pockets are no longer bottomless. Only a certain amount of money, its quantity known with some precision, is available. Like any prudent father, the government would doubtless set aside a store of money to cope with emergencies, but there is no way of knowing how large this store ought to be, how wide a margin of safety would be required, or what the effect might be if investors and the public knew for a certainty that the Fed was capable of running out of money.

Financial emergencies are complicated affairs and there is no way to anticipate their courses; to meet one in perfect safety would require an enormous withdrawal of funds from circulation. Since a gold-backed currency is locked in rigid ratio with the nation's supply of gold, such a withdrawal would act much like a reserve requirement at a bank, proportionately curtailing the nation's ability to go about its business. This new deficit could be made up by fresh purchases from abroad, but such purchases open up some fascinating problems.

Under a gold standard, the currency is out of control. An emergency is not required to produce a deflation; deflation of the currency is built into the gold standard. It comes into play when privately issued negotiable instruments are cashed, and it comes into play again when the multiplier effect makes itself felt through the operation of the Euromarket. As matters are presently ordered, the multiplier effect, by creating large new dollar-denominated obligations abroad, results in an inflation of the currency. With a gold-based currency, however, the effect is deflationary, since the money supply is finite, and any such deflation further erodes the national patrimony, requiring purchases of gold.

With certain modifications, then, a return to gold places the government in the position of the Hunt brothers at the time of the silver play. In order to link the currency with gold, the government would have to behave as though it had obtained a worldwide corner of the metal. Because such a corner is impossible, the Hunts wisely attempted to corner silver, where they had a chance, but the advocates of the gold standard don't appear to have given the matter a similar amount of thought. Substantial stocks of gold are held by governments abroad, and somewhat less substantial stocks are held by speculators and investors. The government could declare such private hoards illegal, as it did in 1932, but such a restriction applies only within the national boundaries; the gold market elsewhere would continue to thrive. In order to maintain the appearance of a corner, the government would have to set an arbitrary valuation of such strength—the equivalent of bidding the limit in the futures market—that it would determine the world price and attract gold in quantity. And once the price was established, the government would have to maintain it, which leads to all sorts of unpleasant possibilities. The whole purpose of returning to the gold standard is to stabilize the currency; otherwise the gold standard makes no sense. In order to maintain the price, the government would therefore be compelled to sell bullion when the market price rose and buy bullion when it fell, alternately inflating and deflating the currency in response to market forces beyond the government's control. Gold doesn't stabilize the currency; it destroys its autonomy, and the possibility for mischief is enormous.

It is a pity that contemporary advocates of the gold standard don't understand futures markets; if they did, they might be obliged to trim their sails. Before a government goes onto the gold standard, a considerable period of debate and preparation must occur. A country doesn't go onto the gold standard secretly, by stealth and at night; it fairly trumpets its intentions. But speculators, familiar with futures markets, likewise have their plans, and the introduction of the gold standard offers a wonderful opportunity for a fleecing operation.

The United States doesn't have a corner in gold and cannot obtain one. It can shut down the free market within its borders and perhaps persuade the British and Swiss to do likewise, but a gold market can function anywhere, in Singapore or Macao, wherever there are telephones. And as long as a free market exists, the price will fluctuate, even if the London fix of some substitute is retained, with a profitable new element added to the equation: a government on the gold standard is obliged to defend gold at a single set price, greatly reducing the element of speculative risk. It is therefore not too difficult to imagine a syndicate of traders—such as the one Dr. Henry Jarecki allegedly established to take advantage of the collapse of the Hunts' silver play—combining to effect an ingenious straddle that would drive down the free market price on the eve of Gold Standard Day, while leaving them heavily short in its aftermath, when the government would be compelled to intervene with heavy purchases to drive the price back up. It would take money, but the money could be found—if not from the Saudis, then from the Kuwaitis, or from the Euromarket, or from untapped private fortunes; the possibilities are various. Nor is there anything to prevent such a syndicate from doing it again and again as the opportunity presents itself, going long and going short and playing the Treasury like a trout. Where there is money to made, money and talent will be found to make it.

All this might come under the heading of the usual fun and games—a billion here, a billion there, a little annoying perhaps, but no big deal to a government that has long considered a billion dollars, even a gold-denominated billion dol-

lars, as mere walking-around money. This is to forget that
there is no flexibility in the gold standard; once the price per
ounce has been set by the government, the government has to
defend it. The Hunts planned to index their private currency
to the price of silver, which, as I mentioned earlier, isn't quite
the same thing.

The Hunts allowed themselves some room to maneuver;
by indexing their bonds rather than setting an arbitrary valuation, they allowed themselves a certain amount of essential
flexibility. Moreover, they proposed to amass a silver hoard of
such overwhelming strength that they could control the market and maintain a reasonable price. The danger was always
that they would be hit with vast new supplies from an unexpected quarter, and to prevent this eventuality, they immobilized the nation's silver stockpile. In the end they failed
because they hadn't counted on tea sets and crisis, but the
plan was a sound one. Gold, as they clearly realized, is a
horse of a different color. Approximately $14 billion in ingots
rest in the vaults of the New York Federal Reserve. Other
gold will doubtless be attracted on Gold Standard Day, when
the basis of the currency is changed and the new price is promulgated, but the quantity will be insufficient for the purposes
of control. Other governments will retain substantial stocks of
bullion—which, at a stroke, the United States has converted
into both a commonplace medium of exchange and a bright
new instrument of policy, allowing the French, for example,
to hope for a tidy deflationary killing in the market as circumstances dictate, with the United States again in the role of
goat.

All of these intricate destabilizing possibilities pale into
insignificance when one considers that the principal world
producers of gold are the Soviet Union and South Africa, and
the true size of their reserves is unknown. Meanwhile, the
Saudis are fast approaching the end of their national development plan, whereupon they will begin amassing dollars as
never before, and the dollars will now be denominated in

gold. The great nightmare of any cornering operation is a massive market intervention by an outside source that pours in fresh supplies or a new and hostile investment, and the possibility of such intervention now looms large. With the United States obliged to defend gold at all costs and the Russians, the South Africans, and the Saudis holding all the trumps—the Saudis could, if they wished, also deploy their money as a weapon, simply by cashing in their dollars for ingots, causing yet another massive deflation of the currency—a devastating new form of blackmail has just been created where none existed before. By contrast, the nuclear threat is a clumsy and perhaps unworkable one; to employ it runs the risk of destroying the earth. With the United States on the gold standard, it would be enough to employ the scalpel rather than the bludgeon, and destroy the currency instead.

In short, a return to gold is a terrible idea; at best, it subjects the economy of the country and the West to repeated deflations. At worst—and the worst is very probable—it deprives the West of the ability to control events. The probable effects of a return to gold are precisely the opposite of what is wanted. The Hunts were right: if you're going to create a hard currency, silver is the way to do it. At least you stand a chance of controlling the stuff.

The gold standard is a dangerous fantasy. In reality, the villain of the piece is the imprudence of the bankers, and its present hideout is the Euromarket. Our course, then, seems clear. We should return the banking system to the thrilling days of yesteryear, strip it of its ability to create new money (as distinct from new wealth, which is the province of the entrepreneur, the industrialist, and the investor), restrain its lines of credit, require it to build up some reserves, and impose some obvious rules on the Euromarket. It is a tidy scenario, easily held in the mind, and there are only two things wrong with it: the danger of enthusiasm, and the fact that the above remedies happen to be monstrously difficult. We have been mucking about with our finances for the better part of two decades now, trying out all sorts of wonderful new solutions that haven't worked nearly as well as (or in some cases, remotely like) their originators had anticipated. When Lyndon Johnson severed the dollar from gold in 1966 and when Richard Nixon allowed it to float in 1971, all sorts of wonderful results were expected; things almost immediately went haywire instead.

An economy is a complex thing, constantly evolving, and the people who manage the myriad sectors of it are often clever fellows; there is almost always a way around an obstacle. Furthermore, the general run of legislator knows next to nothing about economics and shows no inclination to learn; the life of an elected public servant, in nine cases out of ten, is driven now by ideology, now by experience, now by the cares of the moment, and sometimes by the perceived needs of his particular constituency. Given such an intellectual climate, almost nothing is worse than a solution that seems both simple and attractive—imposing a reserve requirement in the Euromarket, say, or abolishing commercial paper.

It seems, for example, to be a very good idea to restrain the massive concentration of debt that has accumulated over the past two decades, turning a vital sector of the industrial plant into a kind of domestic Brazil that lives by rolling its debt. One might begin by outlawing Fed Funds and treating commercial paper as though it were an issue of securities, subject to the control of the SEC. And, indeed, something will have to be done and done soon. Perhaps that is the way to go about it, but imposing restraints on the sources of credit ignores the fact of the existing debt and its central role in the continued life of large segments of the economy; unless a way is found to reschedule that debt (and to do so without bankrupting the lending institutions), restraining credit is an excellent way of making things go smash rather swiftly, and with a shuddering fall.

The chance that the government will impose Euromarket reserve requirements and bring the multiplier effect under a measure of control is unfortunately slim. It is an excellent idea, with predictable effects and long precedent in domestic banking to guide and comfort us. Unfortunately, since the departure of Senator Church from Congress, almost no legislator in this country or abroad gives the faintest indication of understanding the Euromarket or even knowing that it exists. It is a complicated subject, not easily mastered, and the outline in this book gives only the sketchiest suggestion of its dimensions.

Even if a measure of enlightenment is achieved, one is up against not only the banks—whose love for the market burns with a refiner's fire—but the Federal Reserve itself. With some justification, the banks have persuaded the Fed that their activities in the Euromarket must remain cloaked in secrecy, lest they reveal vital information to their foreign competitors, whose governments and central banks are equally protective. Even though fully 70 percent of the balances in the market are denominated in dollars, it can be quite plausibly and correctly argued that the unilateral imposition of a reserve requirement on the U.S. participants would place them at a serious competitive disadvantage.

What is needed, then, is a new international banking convention that would place uniform and flexible reserve requirements on all banks that participate in the market. It is a task of formidable complexity, considering the number of governments to be persuaded, conflicting national interests, the diversity of the banking systems involved, and the need to create either a central clearinghouse or a means of synchronizing the activities of a variety of national regulatory bodies. Even if all this were achieved, there is nothing to say that the Euromarket won't simply pack up and move to Nairobi; like a futures market, all the Euromarket really needs is a telephone line, and it can go into business anywhere.

The rather surly mess into which we have fallen is not so much the result of blind economic forces shouldering their way through the decade like so many golem, but is at least partly the consequence of the conscious decisions and unconscionable blunders of a handful of men pursuing their own gain, obedient to what Dr. Jarecki once told a congressional committee was the noblest of human motives—greed. Well and good, and they cannot be condemned for that. It is an old story, and it usually has but one ending: the government is finally compelled to interpose itself between the citizenry and the consequences. At a time when deregulation is popular— and in many cases rightly so—it is ironic that a major public intervention has become essential, but it should come as no great surprise. A democracy is answerable to its citizens, and maintaining the public order is what government is for. It may be too much to hope that the government will also act with care, or that it will act in time.

Glossary

Arbitrage: In commodities trading, profiting from the price differential of a commodity on two different markets. For example, if the price of silver is $10 an ounce in New York and $10.25 in Chicago, a handsome profit can be made by selling the cheap New York silver on the more costly Chicago market.

Asset (banking): A loan.

Backwardation: A price differential that makes an arbitrage possible (see *Arbitrage*).

Bullion dealer: A broker who trades in precious metals.

CBOT: The Chicago Board of Trade, one of the country's leading commodities markets.

CDs: Certificates of deposit.

CFTC: Commodity Futures Trading Commission.

COMEX: The Commodities Exchange in New York, another leading commodities market.

Commercial paper: Short-term notes, usually maturing in less than nine months, sold for the purpose of raising capital from such nonbank sources as private investors, pension funds, institutions, insurance companies, and other businesses. Commercial paper is not considered an issue of stock and is therefore not regulated by the Securities and Exchange Commission.

Compensating balance: A deposit, maintained in the lending bank by a borrower, that consists of an agreed-on percentage of the loan. Considered in earnest of the borrower's good intentions, it also rewards (compensates) the bank by giving it an additional sum of money to lend. The practice is largely confined to the American banking system.

Comptroller of the Currency, Office of the: The arm of government responsible for periodic examination of the books of national banks.

Correspondent (banking): A smaller bank that maintains a deposit in a larger bank, receiving in return certain services (training for its staff, international contacts, purchases of money). Also applies to the reverse: A large bank rendering such services is the smaller bank's correspondent. In international terms, a bank that renders services within the borders of its country in exchange for a deposit.

Debenture: A bond.

Delivery, accepting: In commodities trading, taking physical possession of the commodity being traded.

EFP: Exchange of contracts futures for a physical entity as when a trader exchanges his futures contracts in New York for a quantity of the actual commodity in London.

Eurocurrency: Money that has escaped the control of the government that issued it, such as British pounds in a German bank, Japanese yen in an Italian bank, or dollars in Paris.

Euromarket (also Eurocurrency Market): Founded by the Soviets to prevent their dollar supplies from being frozen during the Cold War and presently the favorite depository for Islamic petrodollars, the Euromarket consists of those bank operations carried on abroad in such a manner as to be largely free of both national and international restrictions. In gross size, it presently exceeds a trillion dollars.

FCM: Futures Commission Merchant.

Fed Funds: Sums of money purchased from smaller banks by larger, money-center banks.

Federal Reserve: A coalition of twelve member banks, chartered by the federal government and charged with the task of imposing order on the nation's financial markets.

IMF: The International Monetary Fund, a transnational lender of last resort.

LDC: Less-developed country.

Liability (banking): A deposit.

LIBOR: The London Interbank Offering Rate; in effect, the prime rate in the Euromarket.

Liquidity: The amount of real money, in terms of actual currency, retained by a bank or a company for day-to-day business and emergencies.

Long contract: In commodities trading, an agreement to buy.

Margin, initial: The sum of money that enables an investor or speculator to gain control of a commodities contract. Except in extraordinary circumstances, it is usually a small fraction of the contract's actual value and, unlike securities margin, it is not mingled with the broker's accounts.

Margin, variation: A sum of money, determined by the movement in the daily price of a commodity, that is paid by the day's speculative losers to the day's speculative winners. Thus, when the price moves up, the holders of a long position (the longs) profit at the expense of the holders of a short position (the shorts). When the price moves down, the reverse occurs.

Multiplier effect: The mechanism by which a bank, through issuing a loan, inflates the currency.

Negotiable certificates of deposit (CDs): Interest-bearing instruments, originally issued in denominations of $1 million or more, that are sold by banks for the purpose of raising short-term funds. Since they can then be resold by the purchasers, they amount to a private issue of currency.

Offsetting position: In commodities trading, the assumption of a contract that effectively wipes out a previous obligation. That is, if a long position is liquidated, the speculator might assume an identical short position. This not only offsets the old contract but prevents the speculator from ending up with, say, a carload of potatoes (or whatever) parked on his front lawn.

Open interest: In commodities trading, contractual positions that have not been offset.

Prime rate: The rate of interest that banks charge their best (and therefore, largest) customers. Smaller customers are almost invariably charged at a higher rate.

REIT: Real Estate Investment Trust; a legal device whereby small investors could pool their funds for the purpose of participating in large real estate transactions.

Roll forward: In commodities trading, the opposite of offset. A roll forward is the assumption of identical new contracts when the old contracts come due, preserving the trader's position in the market.

Rollover: Moving a time-limited financial or commercial instrument—a certificate of deposit, a commodities contract—forward into the next contractual period without cashing it in or delivering on its terms.

Short contract: In commodities trading, an agreement to sell.

Straddle: In commodities trading, offsetting positions assumed for the purpose of obtaining a tax advantage.

INDEX